35-

Make-Believe
Town

ALSO BY DAVID MAMET

Make-Believe Town

Essays and Remembrances

by

DAVID MAMET

LITTLE, BROWN AND COMPANY
Boston   New York   Toronto   London

FIRST EDITION

The following essays have been published previously (in slightly different forms):

"Gems from a Gambler's Bookshelf" (*Playboy,* January 1994)
"Girl Copy" (*Allure,* October 1993)
"The Diner" (Lands' End catalogue)
"Homespun Fop" (*New York Times Magazine,* June 27, 1992)
"Memories of Off Broadway" (*New York Observer,* November 2, 1992)
"Delsomma's" (German *Vogue,* February 1994)
"Deer Hunting" (*Men's Journal,* Fall 1994)
"Greg Mosher" (*Theater Week*)
"The Jew for Export" (*The Guardian,* April 30, 1994)
"The Northern Novel" (*Los Angeles Times Book Review,* October 9, 1994)
"In Every Generation" (*The Forward*)

Library of Congress Cataloging-in-Publication Data

Mamet, David.
  Make-believe town : essays and remembrances / by David Mamet. —
1st ed.
       p.   cm.
    ISBN 0-316-54340-3
    I. Title.
  PS3563.A4345M35   1996
  814'.54 — dc20   95-53147

10 9 8 7 6 5 4 3 2 1

Published simultaneously in Canada by Little, Brown & Company
(Canada) Limited

Printed in the United States of America

THIS BOOK IS DEDICATED TO
HARRIET VOYT

"A boy has never wept, nor dashed a thousand kim."

— ARTHUR FLEGENHEIMER

CONTENTS

Eight Kings

My house was renovated by two German craftsmen. The elder had been in the military, and he spoke to his associate with military cadence and tone.

I learned that *eins zwo* was, like our American five-niner, a corruption in the aid of clarity. Nine/five and *eins/zwei* sound potentially too similar when shouted, or spoken through static on the radio.

I enjoyed their work songs, the swing of their "Unrasiert und Fern der Heimat," the German military song to the tune of the Russian "Stenka Razin," and obviously inspired by the similarity of the two words *raziert/Razin*.

Enemy troops, prisoners, learned the song from their captors or captives; and, finding only the one point of similarity, elaborated that point into a composition of their own. They built on the one thing they knew, the similarity of the two words, and the song grew like a neurosis, or a bureaucracy — it "organized."

There is a secret sign language of railroad switchmen used in shunting cars in the yard, a hand-and-arm semaphore.

There was the hobo alphabet of chalk marks and the arrangement of stones, "Easy Touch Here," "Mean Man, Nice Woman," "Stay Away."

The New York homicide detectives showed me a code of gestures for Irish, Jewish, African American, Hispanic, man, woman, child.

Knife traders at the Courthouse Square say of a tight-fitted pocketknife, it "walks and talks good."

An actor once told me he knew of twenty-seven meanings of the theatrical term "beat."

Thorstein Veblen wrote that any profession with a preponderance of jargon was make-believe.

But I love and have always loved jargon, the secret symbols, the fraternal hailing-signs, the code of the personals column, the bridge-cheat's recognition signs, the med student's mnemonic "On Old Olympus's Towery Top," and the magician's, "Eight Kings Threaten to Save." To study anything else seemed to me like work.

It was and is of the ultimate importance to me that the better poem about the Light Brigade was written by Kipling, that the Buick Riviera's logo derived from that of the Russell Knife Works; that, on the frontier, Russell Knives bore on their ricasso the stamp "Green River Works," and that, in consequence, to do something "up to the Green River" meant to do it completely.

I love the make-believe of the carnival identification "wee-a-zith" — carney-talk for "with" and meaning, "I am part of the Group"; and the cop's "on the job," the confidence man's "Mister Bates."

The codes mean to me that something of surpassing interest was in progress — that something was being done up to the Green River, which River, surely as the Cocktail follows the Abby Singer, exists nowhere but on the ricasso, between the hilt and the choil.

Gems from a
Gambler's Bookshelf

"The martial arts have always stressed spiritual control based on physical and mental accomplishments. Cards lend themselves wonderfully well to this process."

Ricky Jay, *Cards as Weapons*

For years I played cards every day. The game was held in an old junk store on the North Side of Chicago. The junk store was a front for a fence, and the fence ran a game every day of the year from noon till eight P.M., and I was there every day.

One morning, before the game, I'd gone downtown on some errand, and thought to stop in and visit my dad and say hello. We drank coffee in his office. As noon approached, I said I had to go. He asked where I was going. "Poker," I said. "You still using cards?" he said.

Now, at the time, and for some time thereafter, I found his remark recherché, quite overmuch the comment a wise, tough man — and he was both — would enjoy making to his son. "Are you still using cards?" That is, "Do you still require the artificial constrictions of a self-delimiting game? Do you still need a circumscribed arena, and can you not see that the Game goes on around you all the time?"

I got my brains beat out in a lawsuit about a decade back. There's an old Yiddish curse: "May you be involved in a lawsuit when you're in the right." This case taught me the viciousness of that curse. The other side was wrong. It was a copyright matter. They broke our contract, they cheated, they lied, and, had the case gone to trial, I knew and they knew that I'd win. And yet they wouldn't settle. Not for half of what they owed me, not for a quarter, not for a tenth. They hired lawyers to sit, three at a time, in a room to depose me, day after day. They spent sickening amounts of their and my money demanding the production of obviously useless documents and testimonies. Their strategy was: anger, bleed, and weaken him. Which they did. One day I threw the case up and walked away. I shook my head for several years over their — and my — behavior in the case. Why would they not settle — their legal fees cost them several times what I'd have settled for. They knew they had a loser. And yet . . .

There were two kickers in the case. The first is this: Their principal felt offended by me, which I knew when the case began. The second, which I did not realize until the end of my travail, was that she was not paying for her own defense. Her company had just been purchased by a huge conglomerate and, as part of the bargain, they'd given her substantial funds for legal fees and claims outstanding. One of which was mine.

And upon that discovery my mind recurred to a book, the existence of which I inform you of reluctantly. It is *Super System, or How I Made Over $1,000,000 Playing Poker* by Doyle Brunson, twice world champion of that most excellent of games, Texas hold'em. The book's section on seven-card stud is written by David "Chip" Reese, who writes of a cleansing he took.

Chip was in a game with a drunk. He held a pair of aces, and the drunk, after the fourth card, held four diamonds. Chip was an eleven-to-ten favorite to win the hand, but the drunk wouldn't go home. They raised each other thirty-six times, and the drunk caught his fifth diamond, and Chip retired broke. Chip writes, "I learned then that the mathematically correct play is not always the best play." And I add: You can neither bluff nor can you impress someone who isn't paying attention.

I first came across the Old Cat in the book *Maverick on Poker,* a charming and anonymous work of the 1950s supposedly penned by Bret and Bart Maverick, those rambler, gambler television heroes of my Youth.

A stranger sits at a game and is dealt a straight flush.

He bets, and all the money goes into the pot. His opponent lays down a 2-4-7-9-jack of no particular suits and starts to rake in the money. Our friend, incredulous, points to his own royal flush and protests. The other man points to a sign on the wall that reads, 2-4-7-9-JACK is an Old Cat. Nothing beats an Old Cat.

Well, our man goes out, replenishes his bankroll, and later in the night, he finds himself holding that same Old Cat; the natural lock. He once again bets everything he owns. They both go right down to the green. Comes the showdown. Our man lays the Old Cat down. His opponent shows a pair of deuces and starts to rake the pot. "Ahum," our man says. "You ain't got but deuces, and I've got the Old Cat." At which point his opponent points to yet another sign on the wall that reads, An Old Cat is good only once a night.

I found the same story in *Gamblers Don't Gamble*, 1955, by Michael MacDougall, where the Cat is called a Lollapalooza.

My friend Ricky Jay, arbiter of all things picaresque and arcane, drew my attention to an earlier reference, the 1900 *Jackpots* by Eugene Edwards, in which the Cat goes by the cognomen of a Looloo.

What have we in the tale? A conjunction of two pretty good first principles: 1) Know the Rules; and 2) When something looks too good to be true, it is not true; and, perhaps, a third, Talmudic Opinion by our Thorstein Veblen: "Every profession is a conspiracy against the Laity." When you play in the other man's game, you're most likely going to have to pay the other man off. And I will here again refer to those postmodern *Ronin,* the Attorneys, and their cash cow, the Client, and their milking pail appurtenant thereto: the Contract.

All of us have had at least one Old Cat in our lives. For many it has come under the contractual moniker of the Security Deposit. Times may have changed — though I doubt it — but when I was a Lad, the landlord demanded the first and the last month's rent and yet a third month's rent as a "security deposit," held against what were jocularly referred to as "liquidated damages." This meant, as we all know, that when one moved out one was entitled to play out the following charade:

A: I'd like my security deposit returned, please.

B: Well, you'll have to wait until we've inspected the apartment, to determine . . .

A: Fine. Let's go up there now. You will see I have left it in much better shape than . . .

B: No. In due course, our Inspector will . . .

A: But I *painted* it. I replaced the . . .

B: I'm sorry, but you'll have to . . . , et cetera.

I once had an apartment on a building's top floor. There was a two-foot setback outside my windows, tar paper littered with trash. I spent much of a summer cleaning and painting it. I fitted it with a wooden slat floor, and you have beat me to the punch line in your correct surmise. Come fall, the landlord tripled the rent for what he said had become a penthouse with a terrace. I fumed and sputtered in the approved fashion, but it was his game and he was pointing to the contract, and the clause that was just the Old Cat, and it's not for nothing that the story's been around awhile.

As we speak, there is an agency in Hollywood that handles some rather desired talent. They negotiate hard in their clients' interest, in a style that might be described as ". . . one more thing: I get to kill your daughter's dog." And I was doing business and I needed something that they had when the Old Cat came up. I did the world's quickest slow burn as I thought back to *Maverick on Poker,* and paid them off and got on with my life. Old Cat.

There we have two stories about Humility. A theme to which Doyle Brunson constantly refers, a theme on which much of the gambling literature seems to dwell, in modern renditions of the scriptural suggestion that he who conquers a city is as nothing compared to him who conquers his own nature.

But what of the other component of that which Kipling (and my father) understood as "the Great Game"? What of Aggression? The poker sages, if I may distill them, inform us that the game is legitimate prosecution of one's own interest. That we should, therefore, shun the questionable position, employ the time and energy (and money) thus saved in pursuit of any and all real advantages. That, at the table, these advantages may rest in superiority of cards, bankroll, position, information, attitude, and education; and that pursuit and employment of such advantages must eventually prevail, where reliance on chance or arrogance will invariably come to grief. Tight but aggressive.

Herbert Yardley, in his classic *Education of a Poker Player,* distills poker wisdom to three irreducible adages: If you've got nothing, get out. If you're beat, get out. If you've got the Best Hand, make 'em pay.

Which of us has not stayed on, flogging the now-beaten straight in the face of the assured full house? And is this not — and I will leave Mr. Yardley on this sad, sad note — "staying together for the sake of the children"?

Tight but aggressive.

I walked into an apartment in New York, on the Upper East Side. It was overpriced, but I thought I'd give it a look. I opened the door and there before me, down the corridor, was a magnificent and unexpected view of Central Park. So I paid the man off. One year later, when circumstances required me to liquidate the place, I jacked the price up — on spec, and against a falling market — listed it, and it sold to the first prospect, like me, who walked in the door and saw the view. But first the buyer pointed out the market was falling and that the price was much too high. He suggested a reduction; and, heart in my mouth, I said no, and waited, and he paid me off. Tight but aggressive. I had the best hand, and I made him pay. With thanks to Yardley.

There is a stunningly vicious book called *Advanced Concepts in Poker* by Frank Wallace.

He writes that the purpose of play is to win money, and that the educated player should school himself to win *all* the money, that to do this one must: 1) Take every legitimate advantage, of which sub-A) A legitimate advantage is anything that is not patently illegal.

The author, like Sun Tzu in his non–card-oriented *Art of War,* exhorts us to treat our adversaries as if they were our employees, and to control and motivate them to do our bidding at all times. The advanced concept being sold by the book is *super* game control. The reader is advised to make himself the linchpin of the home (or "friendly") game — to maneuver himself into position to choose the venue, the time, the food appropriate at the game. To develop a reputation for service, to create an appearance of impartiality. If, we are advised, the Game forms the habit of referring small decisions to one man, they will be ripe to heed his request to refer large decisions to him, and will, in fact, be inclined to so act *without* his request, through simple force of habit.

The practitioner, we are told, should, for example, bring the food, inquire as to the particular likes and dislikes of each player, and supply them. The players will feel gratitude toward this man. He can, for example, say, I'm going to get the cigars you, Dave, like, so I will be late. Could we not play at nine rather than eight? Who could refuse him? As this man becomes, in effect, the game's "parent," decisions as to conduct-of-play will be referred to him. Why should they not? Everyone else at the table is out for himself. Our Hero is the only one who has demonstrated that he can behave magnanimously and impartially. This person can now, from "cover," as it were, exsanguinate the home game. And the way to do it, we read, is like the old saying about boiling the frog. Don't you put your frog in the hot water, he'll hop out. Put him in the cold water and turn the heat up real, real slow.

If the behavior above described seems transparent, I, having once been that frog, can only report that, correctly practiced, it is effective in the Extreme, and, as Job's messengers said, "I only am escaped alone to tell thee."

I played over many years in a rather high-stakes home game. One day a stranger, Young Lochinvar, came out of the West all smiles and service. He asked if he could sit in. He told a good story, he brought the groceries, he went out of his way to bring so-and-so's favorite cigarettes. Quite soon we members of the old Home Game were deferring to him. It took over five years and an amount of money both sickening and embarrassing to remember to face the fact we had been had. And then all that money was gone, and we'd been shown up to ourselves, and the twenty-year-long game broke up.

Why did the game break up? Lochinvar had revealed to us that we were not playing Poker, which, like War, can have but one legitimate aim — no, we'd been engaged in a most enjoyable Club and *calling* it Poker. There is a name for the club in which we'd been engaged. It is called the Home Game; and Lochinvar had most assuredly read the book on the home game, and he had practiced it by the numbers, and it bust us out.

Near the end of our game he called me and said that
he was concerned about my style of play, and worried
about my losses. He asked if we could get together, and
we did. He coached me for the better part of an afternoon and made suggestions that in fact did improve my
play. At the end of the session I thanked him, and he
said I was most welcome. Now, my play improved. But
what, I ask you, was my attitude at the table toward this
man, this Mentor, who cared enough to seek me out in
my disgrace? Pretty smart fellow.

So Lochinvar's lesson, in the Great Game, was: Call
things by their name. That was the Advanced Concept
of Poker.

A further lesson might be: If you're going to be in
charge, *be* in charge. I here refer the reader to what may
be found to be a good book on poker: *Home Dog* by
Richard Wolters.

His observations on the retriever are, I think, applica-
ble to behavior at the Game. While teaching the puppy to
sit/stay, he suggests, walk away a few feet. After a short
while the pup will become fidgety and want to come to
you. Just before he does, say, "Come."

One trains the dog by being smarter than the dog, by
anticipating his needs and using his pursuit of them to
accomplish one's own goals, and, thus, both triumphing
and avoiding that least thrilling of Family Observances:
finding out who's boss.

Yardley says, Look around the Table. Find out who's
the Victim. If you can't tell, it's you.

And so I recommend the Literature. It will inform

you to be humble, be aggressive, and, in the book by that genius who may or may not have been named S. W. Andrews, be *wary*.

In the small game, and in the Great Game, the wisdom in these books will, unfortunately, only be appreciated after one has suffered sufficiently to acquire it independently, but there you have it.

Businesspersons got all giddy in the decade now past over Musashi, Tesso, Sun Tzu, and other Oriental strategists and warrior-sages. But I cleave to the books above. To which I add that of Thomas Preston ("Amarillo Slim"), who wrote of a game in Arabia. He was asked, and he came. But before the game, he writes, the Big Boys came to his hotel and asked for 25 percent of his take in exchange for protection, and insurance that his winnings would be collected and paid to him. I remember reading this bit as a child, and I expected the next paragraph to reveal his rage and indignation. But Slim tells us he thought not at all, and accepted their terms. His lesson is that one hand full with quietness will beat two hands full with vexation of spirit, which lesson has served me well every time I remembered to remember it.

My last citation will be from that Mr. Andrews, who, at the risk of blowing the gaff, was the premier card manipulator of the Victorian and, perhaps, of any other age:

In offering this book to the public the writer uses no sophistry as an excuse for its existence. . . .

It may caution the unwary who are innocent of

guile, and it may inspire the crafty by enlightenment on artifice. . . .

But it will not make the innocent vicious, or transform the pastime player into a professional; or make the fool wise, or curtail the annual crop of suckers.

I personally belong or have belonged to several of the groups referred to above. I am now close to the age at which my father was when he asked me if I still was gambling with cards.

I seem, in fact, to have stopped gambling with cards. I think back over those years when Poker was, if not the most important, arguably the most exigent thing in my life. I recall some few instances of triumph, and many of its opposite, and I reflect that "learning the hard way" is a lead-pipe tautology. Trust everyone, but cut the cards.

Bonne Chance.

Sex Camp

One day, after twelve years of school, I was apprised of the existence of a college in New England brave and bold enough to dispense with the traditional dross of the education process. This school, I was told, had no grades. It had no classes as such: All students designed their own courses of study in conjunction with their advisors and then pursued these courses at their own speed.

I sent for and received enrollment information, and learned that indeed, the school was just as had been represented. I was told, further, that far from being an unstructured, laissez-faire institution, it was the paradigm of classical education. I was told — and as I read, I saw that it must, of course, be so — that a school is nothing more than Teacher and Student. And I saw that, yes, as the brochures said, yes, a person of great commitment and maturity — one, in short, who did not require the artificiality of grades but was, in the phrase of the time, "inner motivated" — had, at this school, a deep, true, real education offered to him.

Bravest of all, this school, in eschewing the artificial, had dispensed with requirements for admission. Applicants, I learned, were to present themselves for an interview and speak, for some time, with a member of the faculty; and if both felt it would be "a good mix," well, then that was that. I went East to the interview. I thought that during this interview the Politics of Freedom might serve as the organizing principle for a philosophy capable of explaining my previous dismal school record.

But my forensic skills never came into play. And my quote from William Morris, "The man who cannot weave a tapestry while composing an epic poem is not worth his salt," or some such, went undecanted.

What did we discuss? I don't remember. I remember the beautiful New England hills and the beautiful girls in Frye boots; and that, four months later, I enrolled. I discovered then that my so-easy acceptance had not been affected by the faculty member's sense of my innate worth; neither had it been a fluke. No. Like had found like, and I'd landed not in a utopia of Stoic, self-directed scholars, but, rather, in the midst of a community that had no interest whatever in education.

Well then, one might wonder, how did one while away the hours between dawn and dusk?

In sex, I found, and drugs. I had landed in sex camp.

It was 1965; and the unbelieving faculty and the unbelieving student body dwelt in an Eden of indulgence.

The unanimity of our support for Progressive Education knew no bounds. For neither the teachers nor the students were about to rat the other group out. Like the folks at Harvard, we had arrived, and had found it good. But surely, my father would ask, there are some classes.

"No," I would respond. But surely there are some tests. No. There were supposed independent studies to be mapped out and pursued under the tutelage, et cetera; but both students and faculty, discovering that there would be no repercussions attendant on abandonment of this last potential connection to education, left the meetings off. What persisted? The Journal.

It was the heyday of the Journal. In the absence of tests, in the absence of grades, and as a proof of the existence of independent study, each student was required, to graduate, to submit a Senior Study, and this study took the form, most often, of the Journal. But how rudimentary, you may ask, could this journal in fact be? I will tell you. One semester, the college constructed a small guardhouse at the entrance of the grounds. There had been some vandalism and petty theft, and they thought it good to protect college property. So there was a commotion in the body politic, and the subject of the Guardhouse, as a symbol of repression, came up in the mess hall and in the school paper — I digress for a moment to discuss the masthead of this paper.

The new student editor of the paper thought the layout dull; so he adorned the first page with a detailed drawing of what he informed us was his own penis. But the Guardhouse, I say, occupied our thoughts those days. For we were like the Israelites who had left the bondage of their parents' home for freedom. We complained of hunger and the manna fell from above; and when we complained of the predictability of our diet, we received quail, and again, we complained. And, in this period, we complained about the Guardhouse. One night it burned to the ground.

And when it came time for me and my peers to graduate, we handed in our various journals. My roommate's consisted of the trains of thought that led him first to torch and then to reveal his burning of the Guardhouse. And he graduated.

For, just as everyone who could raise the dough was admitted, everyone who had the dough to stay the four years graduated. Some went, as you may imagine, both kicking and screaming; but all went in possession of a B.A. of some unspecified sort. For it would have been arbitrary to reduce Independent Study to an approximate description of the area explored.

We were brought together — as perhaps they are at Harvard — by our knowledge of our superiority; and we were brought together by the venereal diseases that we shared.

A newly hired school nurse rose in the mess hall to suggest that, as the school was swept regularly by these diseases, it would be a good idea to wear condoms even in the cases where some alternative form of contraception was employed. She was laughed to scorn and spent the brief remainder of her career at school being held in contempt as a prude. What did we do when we were not engaged in flirting or intercourse, in acquiring or digesting drugs?

We did nothing. Periodically, we plotted against an administration that existed less in fact than as a fiction conjured by our need for a foil; and we lazed about bored and unhappy.

But I felt myself superior to those trapped in the hypocrisy of traditional education. Until I went to visit a friend at Harvard.

Now, I did not, and do not, know anything about the specific content of or worth of a Harvard education; but, as a seventeen-year-old, I saw that whatever rigors, tedium, or hypocrisy, or foolishness the Harvard folks were undergoing, they enjoyed a benefit we, in the North, lacked; they had not been abandoned.

The life into which they had been accepted would continue after college; and the time in Harvard Yard, whether education or indoctrination, was to prepare them for that life.

When my fellows and I handed in our journals and left school, we were prepared for no society more exclusive than the criminally bohemian.

As an undergraduate, I developed a contempt for institutions of Higher Learning that much experience as a teacher has done little to dispel: and a nostalgia for the red brick covered with ivy. Recently, I saw a newspaper ad for some large Eastern college, which announced, "We Teach Success"; and I thought, Oh, Lord, if you can't teach languages, or music, or physics, or some demonstrable and practical skill, mightn't you leave the kids alone?

Memories
of Off Broadway

When I was a kid in the sixties I lived on the Upper West Side and walked to school through the Park.

My school was the Neighborhood Playhouse on East Fifty-fourth Street (I was studying acting), and my morning walk took me through the Zoo, where I would have breakfast. After school I went to work in the Village.

I worked off Broadway at most of the theaters and in several entry-level capacities. I ushered — the pay was two dollars a night, and, of course, you got to see the show. I remember Irene Pappas and Chris Walken in *Iphegenia in Aulis* and, I believe, Geoffrey Holder in *House of Flowers* at the de Lys as among the plays I saw before I got an actual job.

The actual job was at the Sullivan Street Playhouse, where *The Fantasticks* had already been running since the Flood. I was hired as a permanent usher but in the year I worked there, I rose through the ranks to become assistant house manager, then full house manager, and, eventually, assistant stage manager.

I was a terrible acting student and I looked forward to both the life of off Broadway and the cachet I felt it gave me at school. (Students at the Playhouse were then, as probably now, forbidden to work in the Theater during the period of their studies, but I construed the ban to refer to acting. Since there was not the remotest chance that anyone was going to hire me to do any acting, I was especially proud of my ability to defy the ban.)

The life was pretty terrific, I must say. After school I came downtown and went to the Waverly or the Empire (now the home of the Eliot Feld Ballet) and smoked cigarettes and watched films until dinnertime. Then I went to one of the Village cafés, the Dante or the Reggio, and smoked cigarettes until it was time to go to work.

At the theater I cleaned the house and the lobby, chatted with Charlie, the treasurer, and, in my days with stage management, checked and prepared the props and costumes and swept the confetti from the previous show off of the stage, and prepared it to be thrown yet again over the sadder-but-wiser lovers. I opened the house and showed the folks to their seats — there were, I believe, about a hundred and thirty of them — and during intermission I sold souvenir programs and recordings of the cast.

Franc Geraci played the Mime. He was, during my stay with *The Fantasticks,* appearing in a workshop production of Horton Foote's *Tomorrow* over at H.B., and Robert Duvall played the lead. F. Murray Abraham played the Old Actor in *The Fantasticks* and he was terrific, and they and the rest of the company were more than nice to my incredibly green self.

Jay Hampton was the stage manager. He and his wife, Judy, had a Lhasa apso. When they scolded it, instead of saying "No," they said "Kabuki." Jay taught me how to iron a shirt — I had to do eight for each performance — and he showed me a special method for remembering all the tasks one had to perform during a scene change. For example: "I am about to go on stage to perform five tasks. . . ." It's a good trick.

Another piece of wisdom, the first I'd ever heard about the Life of a Playwright, came from Tom Jones, one of the play's authors. I was nineteen years old, watching the end of the play from just inside the door to the lobby. I heard a sigh, and there was Mr. Jones behind me, looking at the stage and shaking his head. "If only they would just Say the Words . . ." he said.

In those days I used to hear Kenny Rankin at the Bitter End, and the Greats, Bill Evans, Horace Silver, Billy Taylor, playing piano at the Top of the Gate, where the bartender actually nodded to me as a fellow member of the off-Broadway community. Sundays, between shows, a few members of the company usually went to hang out at a bar called Asher's on Christopher

Street — a location I especially cherished as it was across from the Theatre de Lys, where *The Threepenny Opera* had run for those six years so inaccessible to a mere Chicagoan.

The ensuing years jolted me out of all remaining interest in a career as an actor; and, like others before me, loath to leave the Theater, I decided I'd better learn to do something else.

I started teaching and directing, in Vermont and then in Chicago; and a decade later, I was back off Broadway at the Cherry Lane Theater. We were doing my plays *Sexual Perversity in Chicago* and *The Duck Variations*.

I remember Peter Riegert and, again, Murray Abraham backstage at the Cherry Lane between shows on some Sunday. I came barging in, telling some joke, and then, remembering myself, stopped and said, "Oh, gosh, I'm sorry. You guys were probably 'preparing.' " Their response began with wild laughter and ended with the two of them convulsed and beating the floor with their fists as I backed out of the room.

I worked across the street at the Circle Rep several times, and there I got to direct my first off-Broadway play. It was *Twelfth Night* and it featured Bill Macy, Bobby LuPone, J. O. Saunders, Marcel Rosenblatt, Michael Lerner, Trish Hawkins, and Jake Dengel. Marshall Mason played Malvolio, and Donald Sultan did the poster.

Colin Stinton was Feste, the clown, and we dressed

him in a reindeer sweater and a beanie. He played it straight — apart from the togs — and the newspapers, if memory serves (and it should, because I perused them often enough), said he was the best Shakespearean clown in recent memory. I remember the story of Emil Jannings in Hollywood. He's in the cafeteria, and one extra nudges another, indicates Jannings, and says, "That's the guy who can 'act.' " That's how I feel about Colin Stinton.

Asher's had closed, and I used to hang out at the Orange Tree on Hudson and plague Maury Grand to sing his "Guess Who I Saw Today My Dear"; and I'd drink mixed drinks and feel world-weary.

Later I worked with, and occasionally in spite of, Joe Papp over on Astor Place, and this is as good a time as any to air my own favorite Joe Papp story. Joe ordered me in one day and sat me down and gave me a cigar. He said that he'd been approached by one of the television networks, and they wanted him to create and produce a "new kind of show." The show was going to be live, once a week, after the evening news. It was to feature opinion makers and original thinkers, and they were to get together in a sort of free-form colloquy on the issues of the day.

The panel would include, Joe said, Ntozake Shange, Joe himself, a couple of then-rising politicians whose names I've forgotten, and, if I were amenable, myself. The pay, he told me, wouldn't be much, just a couple of thousand dollars a week, but if I found the idea *itself* attractive . . . Well, the pay was lavish by my standards, and the idea of spouting forth, live, in front of the whole damned country was heady almost beyond bearing. Well, sure, Joe, I laconically replied, if you think it's something worth doing . . .

We shook hands and he thanked me for going along with the plan, and he assured me he'd let me know in the next week when the first broadcast would be, what sort of thing I should wear, and so on.

He escorted me out of his office, his arm around my shoulder. As we passed through the office of his assistant, Louise, she called to him. "Joe," she said, "wasn't there that thing you wanted to talk to David about . . . ?" "What thing?" he said. "Some 'thing,' " she said, ". . . uh . . ." She started hunting through papers on her desk.

"Oh. Yeah yeah, yeah," Joe said, as it came back to him.

"David," he said. "There's some . . . There's some rabbi at . . ." And here he named a congregation in Brooklyn. ". . . and they need a . . ." He looked to Louise for information.

"Purim play," she said.

"They need a Purim play," he said. "Could be anything, really, as long as it's on the subject of Purim. Fifty minutes, hour long. Short play. They need a play, and I said that I'd help them. . . ."

"Uh, Joe . . ." I said.

"When do they need it, Louise?" he said. She mimed looking through her notes.

"Tomorrow night," she said.

"Tomorrow night. Just do it for me, would you?" he said.

Joe Papp, Rest in Peace.

Homespun Fop

I flatter myself that I wear the same clothes every year. I am proud to think that I keep pace with the habit, contracted in the 1960s in Vermont, of living with two pairs of jeans to which sweaters and a hunting coat are added in the cold and T-shirts in the warmer months.

My vanity is pleased by the twenty-year-old L.L. Bean dirty bucks that rest in my closet and by the worn Pendleton shirts hanging above the bucks. And it pleases my vanity to think that neither age nor a wider circle of operation has altered the simple habits of my youth.

But like the gambler who cannot admit, even to himself, the extent of his debts, I am incapable of perceiving, let alone admitting, the extent of my wardrobe.

For I am not that simple American guy who lives in

his flannel shirt, with never a thought to his raiment. Nor was I during my youth. I was, and remain, a fop.

While a young collegian, I learned that everything is accepted in Bohemia save nonconformity, and I shed those idosyncratic articles of apparel in favor of the uniform of that day.

That uniform was enshrined in the 1970s by Ralph Lauren, and he received his inspiration in the same place we Vermont youths received ours: the small-town used-clothing store. When we walked out of our store, we were five or six dollars poorer and indistinguishable from today's fellow or gal in Polo, Timberland, or J. Crew catalogs. Our clothes spoke of traditional work in the outdoors. And well they should have, for actual farmers had sweated into them.

When I was a kid, men did not think of dress. Businessmen wore nothing but white shirts, and no man had yet thought to have his hair "styled" — one went for a haircut, and one thought no more of style than one would have at an oil change.

But I left the 1950s for the 1960s, and Chicago for the counterculture, and learned two things: that one could manipulate one's appearance for real or potential advantage, and that one could delude oneself into considering it something other than personal vanity.

My two-jeans-and-a-flannel-shirt self-delusion followed me from college to salad days in a hundred odd jobs and the beginnings of a career in Chicago theater. I dressed myself out of the old-clothes bins at the Goodwill Industries resale shops. Honest worker that I was,

I paid twenty-five or fifty cents for each article of clothing — the Harris Tweed sport coats and overcoats, the old flannel and broadcloth shirts, all of which were my uniform in those years. I paid, I say, next to nothing for the above, and then spent a fortune having them altered.

I would, for example, take in a tweed jacket and instruct the tailor thusly: I want it taken in at the waist. I want the center vent sewn and a small tuck taken in at the bottom of what was the vent, so that the jacket will not "rooster tail." I want the placket for the cuff buttons closed, and I want the cuffs bound in not more than one-half inch of supple brown leather. I want the collar-piece covered in the same brown leather, and I want patches of the same on the elbows; those patches have to be more rectangular than oval.

And through it all I would assure myself that I was simple, honest, et cetera.

Once, during a brief career as a photo model, I bought and had recut an old Brooks Brothers seersucker three-piece suit. And I had a wide-stripe blue-and-white shirt, with a high, stiff plain white collar. And I must confess I bought what for me was that most questionable accoutrement, a bow tie. And bear with me as I relate the straw boater that I bought and the shameful finale — shameful not in itself, I admit, but in a two-pair-of-jeans sort of guy — a walking stick. I carried, in this drag, a walking stick.

I made the rounds of the photo agencies that very hot summer, which was probably 1970 or 1971, looking, I suppose, like a cross between Tom Wolfe and Lou

Costello. Until I opened the door of one agency and announced myself to the receptionist, who became taken with the giggles.

And I was reminded of what, as Tolstoy informs us, Napoleon feared above all: He feared *le ridicule.*

My other encounter with Demon Ridicule occurred in the same city, slightly later, and concerned hair.

As a kid, I, along with most boys at the time, wore a crew cut. I hated the crew cut. I have a head shaped like a block, and I thought the crew cut made me look stupid.

When I went to college, I let my hair grow long. It did not grow, as was the fashion in those days, to the shoulders, because it could not at the same time allow me to wear a hat. I have extremely thick hair, to which nothing much whatever can be done. When my hair grows past my ears, it flips up, causing me to resemble a water buffalo.

When I entered the work world, I saw the laxity of the East would not do at all in Chicago, and I cast about for a barber. I found a fellow who kept my hair thinned-out looking and acceptable, if somewhat nondescript.

He cut my hair for several years, once every three weeks or so, and in the above-mentioned nonstyle. One day, he asked me if he could "try something new." He had just had a brainstorm, and would I experiment along with him? Well, I submitted and was treated to the surprise of a new appearance. The barber had cut my hair and then slicked it back, with a vast amount of super-strength preparation. Slicked it back, so that it flowed from my hairline to the back of my neck in one ironed-looking progression.

He had cut the sides short and feathered the edges around my neck. When I got over my shock, I was surprised and a bit frightened to see that I actually liked it.

The new hairstyle, for it could not be considered a haircut, made me look dangerous. Yes, I thought I looked dangerous and Italian, or at least Mediterranean. I thought I looked *mean*.

I paid the fellow and hurried out to a local pub, where, in the early twilight, I found, as I thought I might, several of my cronies. I took off my hat, and one acquaintance stopped in the middle of a joke he was telling and said, "Oh, I see you've found Richard Conte's hairdresser."

I made it back to the barber just as he was closing and convinced him to undo what he had done. I then found another barber and reverted to that crew cut I wore through my formative years, and from which I doubt I shall again diverge.

For the crew cut, you see, is an *honest* haircut. It is the haircut of an honest, two-pair-of-jeans working man — a man from Chicago, a man without vanity, whose being stands without need of either introduction or apology. That blue-jeans sort of guy is me. And when I later left Chicago for New York and a wider sphere of operations, I saw that my frequenting the old-clothes shops and the subsequent tailors was an affectation not in keeping with my sartorial innocence, and so I let the habit fall.

And I proceeded to take the old clothes I had left to various expensive New York tailors and instruct them how I wished those old clothes copied, so that I could retain both the fashion and the spiritual purity of my youth.

Girl Copy

I sat for a year in a cork-lined office and looked at photos of naked women.

I did it for a living.

I got the job at a party given by a friend of a friend.

A man came up to me, he said he knew my plays, and asked me to come work for him as a contributing editor of his men's magazine.

I told him I had no idea what such a job might be supposed to entail. He said my duties would be these: to come to the office and offer innovative solutions to various problems, and to suggest projects of my own.

This explanation left me no better informed than I had been prior to my question. "Look," I said, "I don't want to mislead or disappoint you. I am not a good 'company' man, I've never worked on a magazine before, and, though I'm flattered by your offer . . ."

I went on in this vein for a while, warmed by my own candor, until he stopped and assured me that there was nothing in the job beyond my capabilities, that I could make my own hours, and that he would pay me $20,000 a year.

The magazine took up a floor in the Playboy Building.

It was decorated in an informal but serious style; and that, of course, was the manner in which we were supposed to function while in it.

We contributing editors, men and women in our twenties, were being paid to pitch in and be witty and creative promptly, and in service of the Issue and its deadlines.

I wrote my share of letters to the editor. Each letter, either through agreement or through disagreement with the policies of the Rag, was to function as entertainment; and I and the others strove to make it so. We cranked them out, and made up names and hometowns for our faithful correspondents, checking the telephone books of those hometowns to insure that each burg housed at least three people of the name we had appropriated. This tactic, the legal department informed us, lessened the chance of a lawsuit by someone who felt offended seeing his name borrowed by a girlie mag.

I wrote captions for cartoons. Who would have thought it? I'd always assumed that a cartoonist dreamt up the idea whole; but, however it came about, there were these drawings of folks in what would prove to be a comic situation after the caption had been applied, and there I was straining to find a caption.

I wrote "service features"; that is, surveys of a particular gadget or service — toiletries or resorts, for example. The items surveyed were, in the main, sold by our mag's advertisers; and these gratuities I found both easy and enjoyable to write. Perhaps because I felt I was dispensing patronage, I don't know.

I wrote puns and gags, and one-liners, and photo captions; my favorite of the last: We had a shot of a house trailer that had been turned into a helicopter; I titled it "Upwardly mobile homes." I talked on the phone to Henny Youngman. I had coffee and croissants with Eddie Constantine; I created the fictitious craze that was supposedly sweeping the swinging North Side of Chicago: strip darts; I invented the American joke. Yes. This sounds like the pompous posturing of a garrulous old Fool — is he so bereft of kudos that he would stoop to garner that owing to the creator of "How many Americans does it take to change a lightbulb? One." Well, yes. I would so stoop, and there it is in print in 1976. Where did I get the energy for these bons mots? For this, finally, this "humor"? The energy came as a counterirritant to the despair caused by my attempts to write Girl Copy.

Fran Lebowitz wrote that as a child, she detested homework; and then she grew up and became a writer; which, she found, is a life of constant homework.

All over the country adolescent boys and frustrated married men were looking at the sexy photos of the sexy naked women, and these men were having fantasies about them.

Here I was, getting twenty grand a year to look at the same photos and create those fantasies, and it felt to me like work.

I would be given "the blues," blue-and-gray first runs of what would later be glorious color spreads of the said naked women, and I would tack them on the cork-lined walls, and I would strive to have fantasies about them. For it was all a fiction, all that stuff; their names were made up, their biographies, their likes and peeves. It was whole cloth, like the letters to the editor. Someone made it up, and that year, that was my job.

I think my personal best was "Katya with her pants down"; and there was also "Anna is a palindrome," but I'm not sure if that was mine.

I did write: "Tolstoy said that a nap after dinner is silver, a nap before dinner gold. Gretchen prefers a nap to dinner altogether."

Workmanlike, as you see.

Others did better. The office consensus favorite concerned French women, and informed us that French women have eyes like chocolate horses, that they wear white socks and harbor a fear of being frightened by an orangutan that has gained entrance to their flat by means of the chimney. I butcher the above-referenced work, with apologies to its author, whose name I have forgotten. The original can be found in an issue of *Oui*, nineteen seventy-four or -five.

No, I never did better than the acceptable "Katya."

I toyed with "London britches" and "London derriere," neither of which ever progressed beyond the title.

I spent too much time staring at the blues — much too much to achieve that effortlessness that, unfortunately, usually denotes lack of effort.

They were my homework. Photos of naked women feigning sexual interest in something or other — their people, the camera, or, in what was considered quite daring in those forgotten times, themselves.

For there were two plateaus, it seems to me, in those bygone days, two Rubiconim, which we approached with utmost caution.

My editor, the bloke who gave me the job, was, by the way, good as his word. He was generous and helpful, and made a point of both aiding and appreciating my efforts. Our editor, I say, would come to this meeting or that, and display a copy of some rival and less prestigious men's mag, and say: "They've Gone Pink."

To "Go Pink," was, of course, to reveal, in a photo, the Labia; the existence of which was, one would think, a secret to no one, but to which photographic reference was felt, in that time, to be Non-U.

We at the mag considered ourselves gentlemen — and -women. We held to the crypto-British, which is to say wry, self-deprecating, view of our work.

We tried to be funny and smart, and put out a book diverting and honestly, if mildly, erotic. What then of this Going Pink?

But the decision was not ours. It came from on high, and devolved upon the photographic rather than the verbal portion of the floor, and Pink we went — the ensuing consequence of which can be seen all around us in the savage immorality of the American Culture and the general falling-away-from-God.

The second Rubicon was Missing Fingers.

And what was the intent and what the effect of That Magazine, Brute that I am?

I am reminded of a passage in a Kurt Vonnegut book. A young man is admiring the centerfold of some girlie mag. He shows it to an older man and says, "Look at that woman!" "Son, that's not a woman," the older man says, "that's a photograph."

And they were lovely, those photographs. And their subjects were lovely, too.

The models came to the office infrequently; and had I jotted down my fantasies about the models rather than staring at the blues, I would have got home earlier all that year.

I always hoped that the gentle collegiality of the office hid a raucous sexual nightlife, and that in time, I would be invited to share it. I looked, through the year, for signs that I was being accepted and, in fact, for signs that such a secret life went on — that the editorial staff, Chicagoan P. G. Wodehouses, when the Lindbergh Beacon went on, turned to diversions worthy of Arthur Schnitzler.

I more than fantasized about it; I *knew* that it happened somewhere north of Division Street and after midnight. And I knew that I was never going to be invited.

For I was an interloper; I was a Ringer, brought in by the kindness of the Editor, and how could I hope to be given the Office to come to a soiree if I couldn't even get my Girl Copy right?

The invite never came. My closest approach came out of my "strip darts" gag.

I wrote the copy, and the photo folks set up a shoot.

We went, at nine A.M., to some studio around State Street, and various people took their clothes off and pretended to play darts, and we drank the warm prop champagne and went home at lunch feeling foolish.

"Yes," you might say, "that's how you should have felt during that whole year."

And looking back, I think that I did, and my Schnitzler fantasies were signals of my anomie.

I wasn't as funny as the people who were funny, nor as sexy as those who were gifted in that way; what I chose to recognize as Fantasy was boring, and my true fantasies never made it past the superego and onto the page.

I made friends with one of the senior editors, and we bummed cigarettes and talked about Poetry.

I rented a room on Lake Shore Drive and saw the sun pop out of the lake most mornings during the Bicentennial summer. The editor still expressed approval of me, and I got offered a gig teaching drama at Yale.

I went to the man who gave me the job, and he congratulated me and said that he'd still like me, at the same salary, that I would only have to work three days a week, which left four for Yale, and that the mag would pay the airfare.

Once again I told him that he had the wrong guy, that

I wasn't worth it, and he once again said that he didn't share my feelings.

I was very much surprised by his interest and endorsement after a year of my work. But it never occurred to me to accept his offer.

So I left Chicago, that most wonderful of towns, and went to Yale to discover that teaching writing was yet one more thing that I could not do.

Now, going on twenty years later, I browse sometimes through old magazines in a bookstore, looking for copies of jokes and gags and my Girl Copy, and I remember those long afternoons sitting in my office, looking at the blurred photographs of naked women.

Greg Mosher

Konstantin Stanislavsky, at the end of his life, wrote about the craft of the director: "I used to think," he wrote, "that the director was like a chef, whose job it was to mix the correct ingredients in the correct proportions; then I thought that the director was rather more like a midwife; and now I am not quite sure at all what a director is."

I, also, am not sure that I know what a director is.

I grew up in the Theater in the wake of and attached to the tradition of the veneration of the director-as-artist. In those days it seemed that a serious piece of theater could not be created without a serious intellectual at the helm — a priest, in effect, to interpret and implement the oracle.

Orson Welles, Harold Clurman, Robert Lewis, Elia

Kazan, were magic figures in my youth. To doubt their genius was heresy, even though my generation never saw live examples of their work.

These men represented, I think, the apogee of the tradition of the director.

This tradition arose concurrently with the adolescence of the naturalistic play and with the birth of psychoanalysis. The age that celebrated *the material* began to wane, and the new age wanted to know about the intricacies of human thought and behavior. The dramas of Belasco metamorphosed into the psychological or spiritual lyrical realism of Odets, Miller, and Williams.

What did those plays require? A director who was both lyrical and realistic.

Well, this is a hard thing to be. And my experience of the American Theater of the sixties and seventies contains memories of a legion of affected martinets whose job seemed to consist of taking the life out of that year's buffet of Brecht and García Lorca. These folks were called directors, and nobody liked them.

They had entered the tradition at the tail end. They knew that directors were historically treated with respect, but they didn't know why. The Theater, ever fashion conscious, kept pace with the general decay of Culture in the 1970s; and bad plays and bad directors found each other and made the breed of each the worse.

The Theater lapsed into this period of *spectacle,* at which point it is momentarily hovering on its journey,

which will no doubt end in barbarity and human sac-
rifice. No longer did the lyrical realism of the plays demand an interpreter versed — or at least interested — in
human behavior; no, the ballyhoo needed a ringmaster.

And that is what the most successful directors were
or became.

No longer was that person hailed who could help
make a play memorable; that person was applauded
who could make a *moment* memorable, who could stage
the banal showily, and this was called "stagecraft."

But my hero was Stanislavsky, and Stanislavsky wrote
that any director who has to do something interesting
with the text doesn't understand the text.

And my hero was also Gregory Mosher, who has been
standing, simply and quietly, over the last fifteen years
of theatrical depravity, and staging good and great plays
with respect for the text, the cast, and the audience.

Greg ran, serially, what were, prior to his direction, the two most moribund theaters in the country — Death-houses, as we in the trade would have it.
He transformed them, first the Goodman, in Chicago,
and then the Lincoln Center Theater Company, into the
best places to stage a show and the best places to see
a show. He made them into, in my opinion, the best
theaters in the country.

His work, both as a director and as an administrator,
was simple. The Artist was of importance, and everything was done for the artist — including, most importantly, the choice of plays.

Greg didn't stage drivel. You might have liked or

disliked a production or a season of his, but like it or not, you couldn't find it trivial.

Greg ran completely counter to the institutional logic of the time. He didn't court subscribers. He observed and reasoned that subscription audiences are the worst audiences. (Go into a theater on subscription night. You will find that the patrons are there because Their Night came up on the calendar, not because they wanted to go to see a play on that night. Going to the theater according to your subscription schedule is like vowing to make love on Tuesdays and Saturdays — it rather takes the fun out of it.) And so he did away with the subscription series at the Goodman.

He found it offensive that not-for-profit theater companies taxed playwrights a portion of future royalties in return for first staging their plays, and so Greg did away with that system at Lincoln Center.

He was, I think, the first artistic director to begin serious interracial casting while at the Goodman; he, at the same time as Joe Papp, refused NEA funding in the light of their proposed loyalty oath following the Mapplethorpe affair. Greg didn't advertise these things; and, perhaps because of that, he didn't receive any credit for them.

He welcomed Tennessee Williams to the Goodman in the last years of Mr. Williams's life and staged his new plays when no one else would do them.

He went to South Africa and worked with South African writers and directors, and brought their plays first to Chicago and then to New York: Wole Soyinka,

Athol Fugard; he brought *Sarafina* to the States and put it on Broadway, and gave the plight of the African townships its first mass exposure in the States.

And he directed plays so beautifully.

In the last fifteen years of his directorship of the Goodman and of Lincoln Center, he produced close to two hundred plays and directed, probably, sixty of them.

I remember his direction of *Native Son* at the Goodman, with Meshach Taylor as Bigger Thomas. It was, I think, his first production on the main stage of the Goodman after his appointment as artistic director.

He read the stage adaptation of the novel and found it tame. So he inquired and was told that the rights were tied up, and that no other adaptation was going to be authorized. He called me up and told me that we were going to return to the novel and write a new stage version, and give the other guy the credit and the royalties, which is what we did.

Meshach Taylor stood up there as Bigger Thomas and told the White race, and the, at that time, largely white constituency of the Goodman, what they were doing to the Blacks and what it was going to get them.

I think Richard Wright would have appreciated it. It was brave and it was vicious and it was no-kidding. There weren't fancy sets, or moving stages, or a "sound design." In *Native Son* there was a scaffolding, and that was it. Play after play there would be two chairs, or a desk, or a park bench.

Now, you may think I'm picayune, but I think, and

Greg thought, that we'd better damn well get back to Basics; and that if the times and the populace and your desire to be well liked all demand spectacle, you, as an artist, had better deprive yourself of the temptation and strip the play down to the ground and see what, if anything, remains.

He never got the credit as a director.

His theaters more than prospered; they *blossomed.*

Many of us, his associates, got the credit, and the fame, and the money. Speaking as one of that number, I found my careerism took me to the movies. I kept coming back to Greg with a new play or a new idea, and he always said "Sure."

(He didn't say "Let me see it," he said "Sure," and asked when I wanted to do it, and blocked out the time, and then usually asked if he could read it, or if I could tell him what it was about.)

He staged *Our Town* on Broadway, and generations (myself included) who had grown up to think it a jejune exercise found it a masterpiece, and found ourselves sobbing at the simple text and the simple production.

He didn't get any credit for it. He didn't get any credit for his beautiful productions of my plays; he gave the other directors at his theaters the money gigs and the flash gigs. He didn't get the press. I don't think he loathes the generality of the theatrical press any less than the rest of us; I do think he finds it less than elegant, feeling that way, to court them.

He is the Masked Man of the American Theater.

We both recently attended a very elegant dinner party

in New York. The party was in honor of a British theatrical personage. Speeches were made in his behalf, and the personage got up to respond and did so graciously. But he could not rid himself of the bred-in-the-bone British sense of superiority to their American theatrical cousins.

He spoke of the possibilities of the American stage, and how we were *so close* to having a great theater. And, finally, his speech had a whiff of "and soon I will pass among you with mirrors and beads, and trade for your charming Native Crafts." He suggested that we might do exciting plays and attract an excited audience, and support each other and so on.

And through his speech I kept looking at Greg, sitting in the corner. He'd done it all. Not once, but twice — he created and ran two great American theaters, and they were the Good Old Days.

Delsomma's

New York, to me, was Delsomma's Restaurant. Forty-seventh Street, just the right side of Eighth Avenue. In a period of marital interregnum I took a friend there. She and I both wished to keep a low profile, and were not supposed to be in New York City at all.

Mel, the headwaiter, greeted me, "Hey, Dave, how you doing?"

I said fine, and introduced the young woman by a false name. "We're meeting some other people for dinner," I said. "Could we have a table for four?"

He nodded, and took us to a secluded table for two in the corner, and sent over a bottle of champagne.

Yes. That was the joint. Across the street and down a bit from the Barrymore Theatre. *A Streetcar Named Desire* opened at the Barrymore December 3, 1947 —

three days after my birth. Some thirty years later, my play *American Buffalo* opened there, and I was at lunch, dinner, cocktails, and most of the balance of the day, at Delsomma's. John and his brothers, the owners, had been there in the Theater District for forty years, serving superb Italian food and strong drinks. They accepted me as a regular, and I sat, afternoons, at the banquette by the bar, drinking coffee, smoking Camels, and scribbling changes on my play — an intense and perfectly happy young man.

My love affair with the joint lasted over fifteen years and many shows. John would come out from the kitchen, the apron stretched over his belly and a vast cigar in his mouth, give me an *abbrazzo*, and ask me what I wanted to eat. It always gave me a kick. The old waiters knew not to hand me a menu. If a new fellow did so, John, on coming out, would brush it aside, shrug at the guy to say "Learn a lesson," and ask me, "What'd you want today?" Then we'd discuss it, for all the world like two characters in a Hemingway novel, and John would stay and chat a bit.

We'd talk about life on the Street — he knew it all. His family were stagehands, and he knew the facts behind the gossip — who was doing what to whom, and what it meant, and how long any show was going to run.

I thought he looked like a Mafia don. I directed a "Mafia" movie, *Things Change,* and asked him to fly to Lake Tahoe to take a small part in the film. He did, and was delightful. And I always asked him to my plays. He

didn't need my invitation. He knew everyone at all the
theaters. And I never knew if he came to them or not.
Being a courtly man, he may, it occurs to me, he may
have come, and found them not to his taste, and chosen
to avoid the subject.

What a guy. About five feet five and built like a
safe. He'd been in World War II, in the Pacific, as a
Seabee. "The army made some landings, and the ma-
rines made some," he recited, "but the Seabees made
them all."

So we would sit around, and talk about the Street,
and talk about life. I'd bum cigarettes from him; and,
in more flush days, trade cigars. And I would think of
Arthur Miller's story. He had published it in *Esquire,*
in, I believe, the early sixties. And I'd read it there as
a young kid. In the story he, Miller, is in some Broadway pub, some tavern, during the run of a play of his.
A man comes up to say hello. And Miller doesn't recognize him. The man says that they had been in high school
together, and they reminisce. The man tells of his life in
whatever business it was he'd adopted. Getting up to go,
he asks Miller, "What are *you* doing . . . ?" And Miller
tells him that he's writing. Gradually the man realizes he
is *that* Art Miller, and his play is Just Across the Street.
The man becomes tongue-tied and makes his awkward
farewell.

Well, it's a great story. It's the Recognition Scene. For
a Writer, it's King Richard come back from the Holy
Land in *Ivanhoe.* And there I'd read that story when I
was a kid, and there I was in Delsomma's, in *possibly*

the same restaurant where it had taken place. Smoking tobacco and scribbling.

And I held so many earnest conferences there; with the director, with the actors, with the various producers of various plays. I sat there, impassioned and outraged and silent for whole *moments* during those many meetings, before I gave the table the benefit of my wisdom.

And I sat there, all polite and interested, with what seems to have been billions of journalists, who all asked, "Do you mind if I turn this thing on . . . ?" Then punched up their tape recorders while I magnanimously responded, "Go ahead," and thought, "Alternatively, why don't you just *listen?*"

So I sat there and talked one sort of pleasing trash to my coworkers and another to the press, all of the while feeling *so* important.

"Where will we meet?" "Meet you at Delsomma's."

Even the food was terrific. John made this great off-the-menu steak *à la piazzanola:* strips of steak sautéed with peas and potatoes, heavy on the salt and pepper, and if you aren't hungry now you probably just ate.

And penne *al carcoiffi,* and *al tonno.*

Yes, the food was good. And the service was good, and the place was friendly and discreet, and, of course, it's just closed.

A month ago I was down in New York and made a date with a friend to rendezvous, after our various shows, at Delsomma's. I'd been out of town a few brief months. When I suggested the place, he said, "Aren't they closed?" And I laughed at his naïveté. How could they be closed?

Isn't it like our reaction on hearing of the death of an acquaintance? "But I just talked to him last week." In effect, how could he be dead when he was just alive?

So age informs us that, contrary to our sentiment, life is a necessary precondition and may, finally, be nothing *but* a necessary precondition for death; and a restaurant that is open must, of necessity, one day be closed.

Well, then, to hell with it. Am I to demand that a restaurant exist indefinitely merely to assuage my hatred of change?

What of it, if a Very Famous Actress once, at the end of a business meeting, looked me in the eyes there and sighed, and said, "Oh, if I could only find somebody *nice*. Like *you*. . . ."

What of it, if I ate several meals there with Don Ameche?

And so forth.

The joint closed. I met my friend on the street outside the restaurant at the agreed-upon eleven-fifteen, and not only was Delsomma's gone, but the *new* place — some exotic name and a zebra-striped awning — *they* had closed, too.

Closed up tight as a drum, and graffiti all over the front of the building, inside of which hung, on the wall, a photo of John and his brothers with Frank Sinatra; *and* a photo of John and his brothers with me.

It's written, "Let the dead bury their dead," to which someone once responded, "Who's stopping them?" With both of which sentiments I concur.

The Theater District has changed since I was a Lad. But what has not? When I was Young, I'd go down to the movie houses on Forty-second Street in the summertime. Admission was seventy-five cents, and one could stay all night, and it was air-conditioned. I and the like-minded would abandon our broiling apartments and sleep through the movies on Forty-second Street. Of late, it would be as much as one's life is worth to do so.

Now, the city's planning to restore the Forty-second Street theaters and make some sort of "mall" or something, I don't know. So there will be a Mall where once we delighted to describe to the unwary that drug-laden hell. Where, previous, the writer himself slept the summer in picturesque comfort; where, prior to that, first-run movies ran first; and, before them, the thousands of stage shows, vaudeville, and legit, of the twenties, thirties, forties. Where Al Jolson himself did the midnight show at Ziegfeld's St. Astor roof, informing the people, "You ain't seen nothin' yet . . . ," where, et cetera.

Well, let the dead bury their dead.

Delsomma's is gone; soon I'll be gone, too.

New York, it seems, is still there.

Although they have taken to putting the nicknames of the streets up on the lampposts, beneath the street names themselves, to wit: "52nd Street — Jazz Alley," "46th

Street — Restaurant Row," and so on — the grand hailing sign of the last stage of Urban Decay.

The buildings are too big. The Theater has been replaced by the Spectacle, the *New York Times* is too self-righteous to live, and, in short, everything is bad.

Delsomma's is closed.

The Diner

There is an old and probably true story of Hollywood. A Producer is hired and comes, at the end of the day, to report to his betters. He informs on several writers: "I hung around outside the Writers Building for a quarter of an hour, and they didn't write a word."

Writing, in my experience, consists of long periods of hanging out, punctuated by the fugue of remorse at the loss of one's powers and wonder at occasional output in spite of that loss.

Writing, to stretch it, is to hanging out as degustation is to the art of cooking.

I hear, as do we all, of those people who spend eight to ten hours a day at their typewriters, and I think, has no one told them of the Nap?

In this Puritan country we have never truly had the Club, and the last decades have seen the erosion unto disappearance of its American descendants the

Barbershop and the Pool Hall, sparing only — in those more fortunate and generally small-town venues — the Coffeeshop.

Those who have not experienced the glow engendered on one's entering the coffeeshop and having the server inquire, "The Usual?" are poor indeed.

For who wants to stay home? We know, for good or ill, that we belong there; the comfort of domesticity may be great indeed, but it is not convivial.

No, the Idle-Hour, Coffee-Corner, Coffee-Cup, where even the stranger may still find himself addressed as "Hon" — that is the place for me.

We've seen and may still see the white-shirted confraternity of movers and shakers at their sacred table in the window of a morning, settling the business of the town. We've seen the waitress chatting up the trucker, the pair having their fight, and the couple previously believed happily married to others holding their first preternaturally innocent conclave.

In larger towns we've seen the budding writer at his or her table, frowning into the notebook; and in the cities themselves, the actor and actress with their flimsy scripts — outsiders all, at home in the diner, coffeeshop, café.

Where *else* would one go? The Lounge seems to have degenerated into the Sports Bar, that is, a spot one can go to watch television.* That is not hanging out; no: We

---

* I exempt the bar of the Ritz Carlton, in New York, its dispensation due to the merit of its avatar, Norman; and the Twin Anchors, in Chicago, "Positively no dancing."

cannot say it. It is a portrayal of leisure in the face of suspected societal disapprobation. This is not hanging out — it is performance as alternative to anomie.

To hang out is to proclaim and endorse our need for leisure and autonomy. How about that. That frantic and forced consumerism of the Sports Bar will not do; neither what has become the muddled and tense obsequiousness of that proclaiming itself the Restaurant. No. You've got to sit there and eat that greasy sandwich.

There you sit with your beautiful plastic-covered menu. If it's breakfast time (stretched by the familiar local dispensation to eleven or even one o'clock; or perhaps our coffeeshop proclaims its hospitality with that most liberal phrase, "Breakfast Served All Day" — that Danton of proclamations, somehow superior even to the cognate "We Never Close") — if, I say, it is breakfast time, we sit and we peruse the card, *although* we know not only its contents but our election from them; for we do not require the information, we relish the privilege.

"I can have whatever I sodding want," we think. "I have but to bid them, and it will appear. Well, in fact, do you know what? I will have eggs." We then continue, do we not, to specify their preparation, and that of their appurtenances, in detail. And the server stands by. Is he or she testy or short with our self-indulgence? To the contrary. They portray their zeal in transcription of our merest whim; and the alacrity of the subsequent repair to the kitchen speaks not of censure for our narcissism but of the desire to be about our service.

Now, isn't that better than the smarmy "Is everything all right?" — that ritualized Restaurant extortion?

And where else is the writer to go? The libraries seem to be closing; there's very little public transportation; one cannot write at home, for those we love might there confound our occupation with Sitting Around and suggest we fix the shower rod.

No. We've got to write, to read, and, to do so, to get out of the house and to get into the coffeeshop. The Olympia at Pike's Market in Seattle; Jeff's Laugh-Inn at the foot of Lincoln Avenue, Chicago; the Athens Diner, Twenty-third and Ninth, New York; Early World, on San Vicente; the Bon Vivant, on Broadway; Rainbow Sweets, Route Two, Marshfield, Vermont; the River Run Café in Plainfield.

We may stop on the way, at the shoe store, bookstore, gun shop, or cosmetics or notions counter, as our tastes command, but we must go in the end to the diner. We, readers and writers, must hang out.

But can we take our computers there? Thankfully not. Yes, I understand that they are portable; but this, like many another diversion, its portability notwithstanding, is best indulged in the home. Please, do not write on them in the Café.

A friend and I were strolling through the West Village streets where for years he and I, both together and separately, had lived in the cafés. Reading, writing, trying to look deep and attractive. At times succeeding. And there, in the correct posture, elbow on the table, head on the hand, correctly shaking the head in disappointment, we saw the Young Writer.

And yes, the hand supporting the head held a cigarette; and yes, he wore a turtle, or mock-turtle, sweater; and yes, he was unshaved; and yes, and yes infinitely but for this: He shook his head not at a coffee-stained notebook, no, but, you have guessed it, at a computer.

We could not credit it. We looked at one another for that brief instant conveying "I thought that it would last out my day," and then we walked slowly on.

I have hung out at Schwab's Drugstore and watched the actors singing each to each. Likewise at the old Imperial Gardens on Sunset, and similarly there glassed the Writers and the Brits. I hung out at the bar at the Old (but not the *old* Old) Second City and saw Nelson Algren there; and at that of John and Jim Belushi, the Blues Brothers Bar of memory.

I was privileged to frequent the Carnegie Deli of old, and was there invited regularly to join the luncheon club of Paddy Chayefsky, Bob Fosse, Ulu Grosbard, and Herbie Gardner; with Henny Youngman at his wonted Shotgun table, over-by-the-door.

And what better place to read? When I was young the Penguin book was British green, and its appearance in the back pocket of another's jeans was quite as much the Grand Hailing Sign of fellow feeling as was the Volkswagen on the road.

I recall the early sixties and Hyde Park, Chicago; Fifty-seventh Street and the Medici Café, where, barely teenagers, we sat all night and drank spiced hot cider, or iced coffee, and heard the folk music on WFMT and read the Penguin novel, and fretted or mooned over young loves — habits that seem to've stayed with me through this much of a lifetime and that instruct me that the young fellow with his computer has the same right to his callow exertions as I did to mine; and may he be blessed to continue happy in the dilatory habit in the Cafés of et cetera . . .

And may the Automobile disappear (except, of course, for yours and mine), and the Main Street and the Marketplace reemerge with their cafés and lead us back to their pleasures of reading, writing, gossip, mutual observation, and whatever else, if such there be, that makes the world go round.

The Northern Novel

I recommend to the reader the works of Elliott Merrick: *True North, Northern Nurse, Green Mountain Farm,* and the stories in *The Long Crossing.* For a while, in the twenties, he lived in and wrote about my town in Vermont. In *Green Mountain Farm* he describes skiing down the hill to the school with his young son in a pack on his back. I know the hill and the school, and when I discovered his books I felt the joy of recognition.

I remember a similar sense of recognition, in my teens, on the discovery of Sinclair Lewis. It was the shock that the life I knew could be the subject of literature. Carol Kennicott's longing, and Arrowsmith's idealism, and Dodsworth's confusion and sense of betrayal were all things I'd experienced. I remember I sat in the library of the Olympia Fields high school and read all Lewis's books, one after the other. Outside, the sun went down too early, and the day was too cold, just as in the books; and we hid our longings and confusion behind the same Midwestern boosterism he described, and went back to the same unhappy families.

I exhausted the school's catalog and began to haunt the stacks downtown. At the Chicago Public Library on Randolph Street, I discovered Dreiser and Willa Cather, whom I denominated the Two Greatest American Writers. Thirty-five years later I still think so.

The Great American Novel was, to me, the novel of the Frontier, and the Frontier was the Northwest, and the novel was written by the settlers' children. Their story dealt with the North, with harshness, and it was written by people from the North, cataloguing the Scandinavian and German experience of immigration: Willa Cather's *My Ántonia* and *O Pioneers!*, Rölvang's *Giants in the Earth*, Frederic Phillip Groves's *Settlers of the Marsh* and *In Search of America*.

Dreiser was of German descent, Sherwood Anderson of Scandinavian. They came to Chicago and wrote of the experience of the second generation. B. Traven was also a Chicagoan and a Scandinavian, and there you have, as Tristam Shandy would say, my Hobbyhorse.

I have always found the literature of our East effete, and prefer the boredom of much of Sinclair Lewis to, as I see it, the triviality of much of Henry James or, for that matter, Fitzgerald. Fitzgerald was a poor boy from St. Paul, and I'd rather hear about that — in some of the Basil Lee stories — than have that longing sanitized and abstracted into the *arrivisme* of Jay Gatz.

I'd rather not have it cleaned up for me. I'd prefer, to get Freudian, the latent to the manifest dream. I am not interested in Art, nor in Fitzgerald's wish to be liked and accepted. The novel of the East is, to me, too pretty — a second-class European experience. I prefer to read about survival.

The second generation, the children of Polish Jews, came to Chicago and wrote such powerful novels as Philip Roth's *Letting Go,* Bellow's *The Adventures of Augie March,* Albert Halper's *The Chute,* and, to give New York its due, Anzia Yezierska's *The Bread Givers.* These books are, to me, romantic, because they eschew the nicety of romance. They are not the Mudie's triple-decker, penned to amuse or even to pay the rent. They are not neat, and do not intend to be neat. They are about death and love, and the struggle for survival in a climate and in a country that wants you gone.

Dreiser, in a rare flight of epigrammatism, begins *The Financier* with a description of the protagonist, as a young boy, watching a lobster and a squid. They are displayed in a tank at the front of a restaurant for the amusement of its customers. The customers are treated to the gradual destruction of the squid. Every day the lobster eats a little more, and then, one day, the squid is gone. It is explained to us that the hero, Frank Cowperwood (the financier Charles Yerkes) learns at the tank the essential lesson of life: that it is a relentless struggle.

But, of course, he could have learned that lesson in whatever land he happened to find himself. The lesson of America is that a restaurant would stage such a show to lure in custom; and that, to me, is the American — the Northern — novel. It isn't pretty, but it's true.

An old show-business adage has it that anyone can find amusement in the spectacle of an actor, dressed as a little old lady, pretending to fall downstairs; to amuse a *comedian,* however, it has to be a real little old lady.

In my beloved novels there is no question of waiting till the final act to see the knife used — the knife is used in every scene. The aura of foreboding is not an effect designed to manipulate the reader's interest. It is the stuff of the novel. It is not added to the narrative; it is the narrative.

I prefer Hemingway writing of his father in the Montana stories, and of Nick Adams in the Michigan stories; I prefer these to his novels, and I think his novels are superb. I love the darkness of Kerouac's *Maggie Cassidy* and *Doctor Sax.* They are, to me, the *real* story, and the Beat experience, the attempt at escape.

Hemingway wrote, "Tell the story, take out the good lines, and see if it still works," which I find the best advice I ever heard about writing; for, to get esoteric for a moment, if the struggle of the writer to describe is markedly easier than the struggle of the protagonist to accomplish, the result must be trash — a paternalistic exercise.

The Great American Novel is, to me, Dreiser's *An American Tragedy.* In it we see Clyde Griffiths strive to be accepted and to "succeed" — to be "American" — and at the end of the book he does not go home sadder but wiser; he kills a woman who adores him and is executed. And that is, in fact, the tragedy of America: that violence takes precedence over love. It took (and takes) the Immigrants to tell us that we live in a violent land; that the violence is not caused by "the other," but is in us all; and that there may be both a remedy and consolation, but that we cannot recognize, let alone enjoy, either, until we correctly understand and frankly admit the nature of our day-to-day lives.

But I overstep myself. The novel needn't educate or correct; the true novel — my Hobbyhorse, the Northern Novel — need only describe. As it deals with American Life and, specifically, the Immigrant Experience, it must be largely an attempt to describe the unsettling.

I recognize the hardships described and the hardship contained in those efforts at description. I know the hill in Elliott Merrick's book, and I felt the same recognition on first reading Dreiser: Yes, that's what it's like, and it's difficult.

Deer Hunting

It is December 13, and there are six inches of powder snow on the ground. It would be a perfect afternoon for cross-country skiing, and in any previous year I would be thrilled at this first chance to ski. This year, however, it's going to take an adjustment, for if it is a perfect day to ski, must it not also be a perfect day to hunt? And why would one ski in the hunting season?

One would not. The hunting season ended yesterday.

And there, of course, were the fresh tracks of a buck mocking my path from the house to the cabin this morning. I knew they were fresh, as the snow kicked up in front was bright and sharp; I knew they were a buck, as I could see the imprints of the dewclaws behind the main hooves. Now, I know that opinion is divided on the reliability of the dewclaws as an index of sex, but this was my first serious season of hunting and so I count myself the heir to any information, any hypothesis that might aid me in the understanding of the deer.

The dewclaws bit was garnered from several of the many hunting books I read before and during the season. The nineteenth-century hunter-writers endorsed, and the contemporary ones derided, dewclaws as a test. My friend Bagwell informed me to look at the register; i.e., the relative position of the front and rear hoofprints. When the rear hooves print to the inside of the front, you've got a buck, as the buck's shoulders are wider than its hips; with a doe, he said, the opposite is true.

This morning's track, by that test, is, again, a buck; and lo, I am on my way to my own mass of fact and misinformation.

My pockets are full of compasses and match-safes improvised from empty shotgun shells thrust one into another. My mudroom is hung with various blaze orange garments. There is the last of "hunter's soap" by the tub, and phosphorus-killing clothes wash by the washing machine. My hunting licenses (Maine, New Hampshire, and Vermont) are in their little blue folder, and up on my desk. They've ridden in my pocket for the last two months. I suppose I should give them a Viking's Funeral and toss them into the cabin stove, and perhaps I will. After this short review.

Bow season started in October. Jimmy at the River Run Café told me that there were deer down by the bottom of his land, and he would put me on a stand. So I went out with him.

I was dressed in about fifteen layers of clothes. My army-surplus pants were crammed with extra knives and hones, with candy bars, and rope. I carried a belt pack that held a camera and film, and a small day pack in which was I cannot remember what.

We went down to the stand, and I somehow got up it. I belted myself to the tree and hauled my bow and then my various packs up, and hung them in the tree.

There I was, a lovely autumn day, Camel's Hump off in the distance, the tyro, attired in camouflage, my face obscured with burnt cork, up in the air, waiting for a deer.

What did I expect? It took all of five minutes, and there they came.

Suddenly, from god-knows-where, there were two deer in the small clearing beneath me. A doe, and what looked to be a spike-horn buck. Now, the season, at this time, was "any deer," and I could have shot either as they walked up to my stand. But I would have much preferred to shoot a buck, and I could not make out for certain, at the distance, if the second was a buck or not. So I waited for them to get closer to me, which they did.

They walked right underneath my stand. Sure enough, it was a buck. And he was standing there, grazing, swishing his tail side to side in what some authorities say is the "all clear" signal.

Heh heh. I had him, and what was this nonsense about the trials of deer hunting?

Then I realized that I was on the wrong side of the tree.

To shoot the buck, I'd have to maneuver my arrow and bow out from the right side of the tree, lean back, and bring them to bear on the left side, without disturbing the deer.

Ever so quiet, I did so. And I did not disturb them, for they walked quite peacefully off, and back into the woods.

It seemed quite a while before my heart stopped pounding.

It was thrilling to see them appear out of nothing. And they were so beautiful walking up the hill. Well, it was four o'clock, and the deer tend to move at sundown, so there I was up in the tree, and I settled down.

I think if you'd like to renew your acquaintance with yourself, you could do worse than spend time on a deer stand. Sometimes the hours go quickly, and you become part of the scene. Sometimes each half-minute is torture, as you strive to settle down. On the stand this year, I had a bird land on my bow and start to hop to my glasses, when his eyes flashed "what in the *hell* . . . ," for all the world like a vaudeville comic doing his turn. Up in Maine I had another bird land on my rifle.

I got to see the sun come up and go down in the woods many times, and the various squirrels and chipmunks. I heard a lot, and began to understand what some of it meant. I heard deer several times. I only saw the two, but I saw them repeatedly.

There I was, up there in the tree. As the sun started coming down around seven, there were two deer, coming back. It was fairly dark, and I was not certain at first that they were the same I'd seen before. By the time I was certain, I had missed my chance, and they were too far in the shadow for me to risk a shot.

I was back the next afternoon, carrying one third of the equipment of the day before. I was up in the tree at three. At four, here they came, up through the same clearing. But this time out of range. And I stayed in the tree till seven, when, again, back they came, again out of range.

And so *that* story went. Several nights, the deer just out of range, and me thinking: If this were rifle season, we would tell a different tale. And Jimmy got his doe, and hung her up at his house, and she looked real pretty. I regretted not taking my shot, but consoled myself that several weeks of deer hunting lay ahead. Then I went up to New Hampshire, for the beginning of the muzzle-loading season.

My friend Bob put me onto what seemed a superb site. There, in a small group of apple trees, was some deer sign. They were eating and defecating there. And there was a scrape. In the rut, bucks paw the ground, and urinate in the scrape, and draw a hoof through it to advertise, to mark their territory. A buck was coming through there, and he meant to come back. So I got out my bow saw and cut down some branches, and put up the stand, and sat up there afternoons, and saw the sun go down in New Hampshire a bit.

Now, what was going wrong? I knew I could sit still; hell, the bird landed on my bow. I knew my camouflage was good; the deer had not seen me. I knew the wind was right to keep my scent from the deer, and I knew they were there. Why didn't I see them?

I puzzled that one out for a while, until I came across a tip in a contemporary book. The hunter-writer had been approached by a friend who had a question similar to my own. The writer had reviewed his friend's apparatus and behavior, and his prescription was "Paint the bottom of your tree stand." For the top of this man's stand was brown, but the deer only saw the bottom, and the bottom was white.

Now, I remember reading that book before the season began and thinking, "What an idiot." And so I thought until I left the stand the last day in New Hampshire, and looked back at what had been the position of my stand, shaking my head, and saw the bright white stumps of the boughs I had sawn off demarking my position in the tree.

Was that what kept the deer off? I think so. In any case, it was a lesson.

Bob invited me to Maine. That's where the big bucks are.

And we got up at four and were out in the woods by five-thirty or so. We'd split up and meet to have lunch. I was Up There in Maine. I liked the sound of it.

Again, I started off carrying much too much gear; but I began to emulate Bob and by the third morning was down to a wool shirt and vest, and moving pretty quickly through the woods. I was looking for tracks.

The second morning I found those of a doe and

thought, "If I can figure out this is a doe, perhaps a buck can, too," so I tracked her.

It was as beautiful a morning as I've ever seen. I tracked her several hours up a mountain. At one point I could see she started running, and I wondered why she would. Then, fifty yards up, a coyote's tracks came in, and he and the doe continued up the mountain.

It was getting to be about time to turn back for lunch, and I was sorry to do so. I would have been happy tracking that doe forever.

I made a fire, and brewed up a cup of tea, and sat there in the snow, by a brook, up on the mountain.

The afternoons I'd generally sit on a stand, over sign; then in the evenings we'd repair to one of the two cafés and check the logbook to see who had brought in what; and check at the reporting stations to look with envy at some rather large bucks (one hundred eighty pounds is big for Vermont; in Maine we were seeing two-hundred-sixty-pound deer). Now, each day, at the end of the day, I'd sigh, and get up from my stand, and start down the mountain, trying to determine how I had erred and castigating myself for those errors: "You were not sufficiently still, you did not accurately gauge the wind, you were not acute enough to observe movement. . . ."

Then I would remind myself that I'd just had about as good a day as anyone is entitled to have — which was true — and that I was learning, and that those things were the whole point of the exercise.

So I would stoically return with Bob to the café; there I'd see the other men, who had taken deer, beautiful deer, and I would be washed by envy and the wish to "get out there" the next day.

And then one afternoon we saw the monster track.

This was a big buck. His hoof was over five inches long, wide, and rounded at the tip. His shoulders were set wide, and if you followed those tracks, they must lead to a deer. We lit out after him.

After a bit, the deer's ambling gait quickened. He knew he was being followed. Bob had spotted the tracks first, so it was "his" deer, and he took off after him. I took a course out to the right in case the deer circled — not a bad bet.

At nightfall — no deer, we met back at the road.

The next morning Bob was back on the south side of the road, where he lost the deer, and I went up to the north. I came across the monster tracks and followed them up the mountain, and lost him up there.

But I'd come across a game thoroughfare, new and older sign of moose and deer; and I inferred from it the deer's daily pattern. So the next day at dawn, I was back on my track, on the thoroughfare.

There were no fresh tracks of the buck, but I crossed those of a sow and cub bear, fairly fresh — I'd missed them by as few minutes as will make the story acceptably dramatic — and fresh tracks of moose. I took a stand, that day and the next, in a high position over the game trail, but I saw nothing.

And that was Maine.

I was flighty, and unscientific, and not sufficiently perseverant; but I'd gotten out there and learned a very small bit about tracking. And had sat in the snow and the rain and the dark, and was having a superb time.

It was now centerfire rifle season in New Hampshire.

I took a Mauser .308 and sat on the ground, up the hill from the scrape I'd found there earlier. I thought that perhaps the deer had had time to forget and/or forgive my solecism with the naked stumps; and sure enough, there was fresh sign.

On the second afternoon I was sitting there, quiet as the bored dead, when I heard *snuffing* off to my right and behind me — this was not a drill — and I thought I would turn ever so slowly, and all that I saw was the bush whipping in the wind and the hindquarters of the deer, bounding into the dark.

He'd (I afforded him the courtesy designation of "buck" — it was too dark and much too sudden to make out what surely were horns) come down the hill, and would have walked right past me. It was three and one half paces from me to the bush. And *what* was I hoping to accomplish? I knew I could not beat him. I *knew* that he had to see me coming around; and I knew that my only chance was an excellent chance: that he would continue down the hill, positioning himself per-fectly, quartering away, close enough to throw the rifle at him, and the wind *still* in my favor. And yet I found it good to turn around, and there was *that* deer. . . .

And it was also centerfire season in Vermont.

Now, I knew where the deer were around my house. Didn't I see their sign every morning? And I knew they went up the hill in the morning, right up from the apple trees. I tracked them back there, just behind a given-up apple orchard and right beside an open field, a textbook-perfect location for deer. In support of which theory, in a small clearing in the woods, there was the first sign and scrape, and the deer were there.

And opening morning, *I* was there, and went out of my house to see a couple of trucks parked up the road; and hunters other than myself had sussed them out, too, and were back in my woods.

I stayed home.

My third great disappointment-lesson of the season happened in a field not far from my house. I knew there were apple trees back there and I'd seen a rub — a mark on a small tree made by a buck rubbing his antlers. There are two sorts of rubs. One is made in the spring, by the buck running the "velvet" off; the other is made in the fall, as he prepares for the rut. This was a fresh "rut rub"; and he was out there.

I tracked him evening after evening, and saw his path, down through the field, over the rise, down into the knoll, and into the woods where he'd made his rub.

It was all right but the wind.

The prevailing, fairly invariable wind blew such that it would be impossible to take a stand above the knoll without also taking my scent to him.

Yes, you have it, until that afternoon.

Well, the wind was correct. I put some "doe-in-heat" buck lure down in the woods, by the rub.

The buck would come down, and the wind would take the lure to him and keep my scent off. The buck would come down the knoll, and I would have an easy shot before he made the woods.

I sat against a tree, just under the crest of the knoll. I practiced mounting my rifle. If he came down, well, then, I had him. He could not see me; he could not smell me. I was quiet, so he could not hear me.

The sun started to go down, and I heard him walking just above the knoll. He snorted twice. He'd gotten the lure. He was saying, clearly as day, "Grace, is that you . . . ?"

And everything was just the way that I had planned. I covered the safety with my left hand and eased it off with my right, and it went *click* loud enough to wake the dead, and he snorted again, in transit, and was heard lighting off for somewhere else.

I would have given, at that moment, much to have an anvil and a maul. For my beautiful Mauser rifle was a worthless traitor, and I was a fool. I fumed.

My last adventures came in the last week. In Vermont muzzle-loading season. My friend Bill Bagwell, a skilled hunter, had come up from Texas. And I showed him the stands, and we sat.

It was late season now. The rut was over, the food source, apples, was exhausted, the deer had been hunted heavily for a month and they'd abandoned their usual patterns.

The stands proved dry. We walked a path, hoping to cut a track, and we found the track of a buck and followed him into the woods.

We saw him go from a browsing, meandering walk to

a determined stride, and then to bounding, as he heard us behind him. We saw an eighteen-foot leap, on a slight downward slope, as he cleared a deadfall that held us up several minutes, and we tracked him to the brook.

Now, this was a real obstacle. He cleared it in one bound, but it was partly iced, and we did not know which ice covered a rock, and which a drop into the water. As we cast up the bank for a crossing, we heard him break a twig. We couldn't see him, but we heard him up there, looking at us. And, when we got across, we saw where he'd stood as we floundered on the bank.

We tracked him till the sun went down.

Bill went back to Texas, and I played out the season on various stands, and, as of sundown yesterday, that was it.

What is the clue? Start early, get serious, learn from your mistakes, give them respect. Lord, they are smart.

I played high-stakes poker at casinos in Nevada for a while; and, for a while, did fairly well. But I will not forget those players with knowledge, character, and experience, the true professionals. One could not trap them, as they were more wily; one could play ploddingly heads-up, and they, being more skillful, would prevail. One could hope to *get* lucky, but their character and skill would get one broke before such occurred — there *was,* in fact, no "getting lucky"; if one wanted to beat them, one would have to study them, get serious, and give them respect.

What an education one can get out in the woods. The wind, the weather, the food sources, and the phases of the moon, the habits of deer, and of the other animals — they can alert the deer to you, and vice versa — are all part of the study.

I saw the ground breathing, on a New Hampshire hillside.

There was a very high wind, and the treetops were whipping. I was on the ground, looking at sign, and I saw what appeared to be the ground heaving up. I blinked, but it continued. I saw it was a regular movement. Up and down. Regular, rhythmic movement. Perhaps there was a bear hidden under the leaves. I stood up and saw that it was a large area, some four or five feet on a side, that "breathed." I stepped back and saw that the area was double that size, and the breathing continued. It was no bear. It was no animal at all. Either I was hallucinating or I'd stumbled upon some unknown natural phenomenon.

My heart raced.

I tried to manufacture an explanation. Then I heard the creak and saw that it was caused by the tree. A birch tree had spread its roots wide over a little gully. The gully had washed out, leaving the roots exposed. They had been blanketed by leaves, and the high wind was swaying the tree. As the top swayed, the roots answered, and raised the carpet of leaves to resemble the process of breathing.

I remembered a story by James M. Cain. On sentry duty in France during the First World War, he had felt the earth "breathe" and had noted it in his sentry log. He felt it, and I'd felt it out there, too; not at the birch tree, but at that time just before dark when it, if you will bear with me, "decides" that the day is done.

If you are sitting still, you see the gradual dimming and change of the woods. It progresses, and then there is one moment, as if a ratchet had slipped, when it is something new; it is not day, but night.

It is as if the woods breathed.

I saw it many times this fall; and got my heart fluttered by what could only be the white tail flickering in the woods up ahead. It was a snowflake, two feet from my eye, at the end of a spiderweb; and, as I watched, a second slid down the web to join it.

Now, at the end of the season, as at the end of the day's hunt, a review seems to banish remorse and to goad information into knowledge, and to gently counsel thanks.

Between Men and Women

When all is said and done, it is, of course, always about sex.

The Lawyers say it starts in bed and ends in court; and indeed, the contemporary barrage of pornography is balanced by our brave litigiousness.

Many seek and live to sustain the feeling of transport that sex sometimes brings, as if one could live in abandonment forever. It is the adolescent drama equivalent to the search for perpetual motion. The child tries to square the circle, thinking, "Many have failed, but I am blessed"; men of more advanced age set out to conquer the world, the land, a skill, one or some women.

And women, for their part, what would they be painting and primping for if not to conquer that same man?

Where, in this seamlessness, is there room for misery?

In the yearning for romance, in the man's Mariolatry and in the woman's hero-worship, in the urge to conquer and the urge to be subdued, in the ironic operations of chance upon the enthusiastic, in the bitter and protracted conversation of remorse.

We are crazed to get into it and crazed to get out of it.

We are unbalanced by passion or by the hatred of the passionate. The only control seems a dry, unregarding philosophy, and such is practicable only by those pitifully devoid of such gifts of spirit as our own. Our new, painful wisdom, when we have terminated the marriage, the affair, the pact, or the illusion, does not prevent us from finding a new partner of such proverbial unworthiness as to send our friends scurrying for the telephone.

Through it all, as audience or actor, we nod our heads sagely, or shake them in sorrow, and know that in spite of ourselves we are fated to square the circle, come at the Hesperides, and live both happily and forever.

We harry the world for novelty until it palls and then must have stability forever, or until it wearies us. In both demands we ape the infant, center of its world, who requires that the world conform to both and each of its two modes: furious and satiated. And, of course, at the same time, we call it grand.

The chance discovery of the old love letter, the personal erotic code, three words or symbols on a florist's card, the note found in a coat unworn these years since the end of the affair — the anger, the self-loathing, the embarrassment, are confusingly sharp, as are the memories of more successful love. Relics of decision and folly are both proved by time to've been operating in service not of our own personal dreams, but of the mating instinct.

There is its stamp, even in the curses of the divorce court, the sex slanders of the popular press, the lawsuits and totalitarian sexual proclamations of freedom: "You have disappointed me. I demand you, your sex, someone, be all-in-all to me, and you have failed. Redress my wrongs, make me complete." The one sex demands the other make it whole, and even the supposedly dry legalistic debate is nothing other than a simulation of the sexual act: "Complete me, release me, make me whole."

And the women can confab with the women and the men herd with the men, as both have always done, and bitch to each other without end, but to consider such affinity anything other than a counterbalance is to confound the racing form with the race.

What could be more lovely than two folks in love, more sordid than two bickering — who demand that not only their partners but the Community make them complete, as if they were, for all the world, returning a defective item to the place of purchase and exhibiting its shortcoming.

As one is. For it was the Group that gave us our choice, and if we are, as we are, fated for bliss, then surely the group, in large or small, must bear the fault.

We love the wedding, but we adore the divorce. Its

entertainment value is protracted through the rift, the threat of reconciliation, the legality, and postmortem recriminations.

The wedding proceeds with thoughtless speed from the courtship (in itself a bore to any but the Two) to the ceremony, and then to the Community wait for and insistence upon the first offspring.

"But no," we, speaking as Principal, exclaim. "Nothing, not birth, nor parenthood, neither wisdom nor age will debar us as participants in the drama of sex." We will claim until death at the very least the honorific right of search for bliss.

Why with one rather than another? The figure, or the face. The intellect, or wit, or this-or-that — we fall inevitably back upon "a certain, indisputable something," proclaiming them the one.

But how often has that something led us astray — like a compass that is sure of North, but whose North bears no relation to any known pole.

And through much of it we have no goal, only a desire for a state — that state which would amalgamate the thrill of the hunt with the torpor of perfect repletion. What a laugh.

I suppose we could strive to maintain our dignity, and some of us do, and most of us do at some time.

That dignity might rest on a sense of humor and, for the odd instance, an appreciation of tragedy and perhaps some belief in its curative powers.

At the end of the day we want someone to hold our hand.

If we are happy, we want someone to be for us and to whom we can be a hero. In misery we strive to be or find a victim.

In either case we're searching for a partner to share our idea of home.

The Screenplay

Screenwriting used to be referred to as "writing titles" — it was a description that persisted as a survival and then as a nostalgic anachronism into the early 1940s.

The old joke has it that a neophyte screenwriter in the early "talkies" era penned: "She comes into the room. She discovers him there, and words cannot describe the scene which then ensues."

The joke, for those insufficiently hep, is this: If words cannot describe the scene, what the hell is the screenwriter getting paid for?

Well.

The screenplay has become the late-twentieth-century equivalent of tatting. Anyone can take a hand at it, and it is accounted "honorary work," that is, it is considered neither a pastime nor an avocation, but a potentially remunerative employment of one's time.

And indeed, it may well be. Those countless hundreds of thousands working away on their screenplay ideas may have their dream come true — for, like tatting, the contemporary screenplay requires only the minutest understanding of rudiment on the part of the practitioner.

If the film is a drama, the writer must be a dramatist of great or less ability; he or she must be able to craft a progression of incidents which progression piques and holds the attention of the audience in the main. But films have degenerated to their original operation as carnival amusement — they offer not drama, but *thrills*. (The early nickelodeon showed a freight train steaming toward the audience, and they, unused to the technology, said, "How real," and were stunned. Today's computer morphing, bluescreen, et cetera, function similarly.)

It does not require a dramatist to "script" a film based on thrills. The requirements of such films are not more elaborate than and, in effect, are fairly identical to those of a straight-out pornographic film — the minimal plot is a fig leaf, like the well-brought-up young woman's first refusal.

Like tatting, or mime, the skills in contemporary screenwriting are accounted difficult by courtesy, and the few variations from the norm are about as innovative as the sartorial accessorizing of the rich.

Perhaps there was a Golden Age of Drama in the movies, perhaps not. And perhaps I delude myself to think that the business was once overseen by filmmakers rather than exploiters. The difference, to me, between those two categories is this: Each wants to make money, but the filmmaker intends to do so by making a film. The endless and byzantine structure of the studio system — like any terminal bureaucracy — rewards the bureaucratic virtue of adherence to the system.

And the system starts with the script reader.

This is the entry-level position: Bright young people, fresh from the hierarchy of the university and the film school, begin here. They are given scripts and understand that they are to endorse the predictable — that any deviations from formula will be made through and by their betters. They are to stand at the gates and reject the unusual. It must be a terrible job. I'm sure it is — wading through reams of printed paper, day by day, that is not only worthless but boring.

In the late sixties the small theaters had made available to them for the first time significant amounts of grant moneys. Where once these theaters were run by and succeeded through the efforts of those who could communicate with an audience, now they were captained by those who could write grant proposals.

Similarly, where once the screenplay was written to appeal to the star or the director — to those who would make it into a film — now it is written to appeal to the bored script reader.

The screenplay of today has, in effect, become a novel.

We have heard "Words cannot describe the scene which now ensues."

Ha ha. But I have read, "You guessed it: here comes the sex scene — I'd write it for you, but my mother reads these scripts"; "He comes into the room and we hate him — we really hate him"; "Outside the window: New York, in all the Vicious Splendor"; and, my favorite, "He turns and walks away from the camera. Nice butt, kid."

The last haunts me like an Escher drawing. It is, to me, the linguistic equivalent of Klein's Bottle, which can have no basis in reality. Let us consider it as an instruction. To whom is it addressed? Not the casting agent. Not the actor, as yet unchosen. The writer compliments his or her own perception — his or her own *thought.*

Similarly, if we consider it a description, we find that it is a description of something we have not shared — the writer's thought, and by extension, his or her ability to think.

It's monstrous.

Can such a phrase help the actor or the director? No. But it *serves the same purpose as* the final film — it appeals to the jaded.

"We hate him." No doubt, as "he" is meant to be the villain. This enormity skips the fact of the film altogether and refers directly to the emotions of the audience.

Now, one might like to be assured that the audience is going to hate the villain — it might make the melodrama more effective — but it seems to me that the task of screenwriter is to communicate to those who are about to make the film *why* we "hate him," and such can be done only through delineating what the actor *does,* and what the camera *shoots.*

Many of the modern efforts at screenwriting contain the "you-know-and-I know" error in describing the characters.

"She comes into the room. She's beautiful, she's tough, she has a pair of eyes that make you think of olives in a plate of milk," or some such. Such description can be written interestingly, but at the end of the day, the beauty, the eyes, the posture, et cetera, of the character are going to be those of the actor or the actress cast in the part.

Similarly, "You know and I know that they've been around the block." Well, *how* do we know that?

"He wants to take her hand — or *does* he . . . ?"

Such makes the script reader's morning a bit less drab, but it is unfilmable.

"The lead car crashes into the bus. Flames envelop the sky. Brad jumps from the lead car into the Jeep, which careens on two wheels around the Volkswagen."

This, of course, is the stuff of comic books. As most action movies are aspiring to the level of comic books, it might be considered good (useful) screenwriting, except for this: The action sequences will be thought out and executed by the director and the stunt coordinator, with little or no relation to the material in the script.

Similarly, the "juicy" parts of the modern screenplay: "Her long legs twine around his back, and the sweat from his . . . ," et cetera. It's supermarket pornography; it might be accounted worthwhile writing if such pornography is what the studio intends to make, *but* the obligatory scene of pretend fornication will take place on the closed set with the actors miming passion in complete disregard of the supposed script. Nice butt, kid.

Altman's film *The Player* contained a scene in which a studio executive explained that the studio was unnecessary, one need only look at the headline of the affective news story and there's your film: "Mother kidnaps, abuses own child," "Bank clerk returns two million dollars." Well, it's so. The housewife in Topeka, and the salesman in Canton, and you and I can write that screenplay. Indeed, most of us have.

But I consider the screenplay drama in schematic. Of late, I have begun to think of my outlook as an idiosyncratic anachronism — like dressing in buckskins, premarital chastity, organized labor, or reading, but I digress. The flickers began, as noted, as an arcade amusement — a trick to extract a modicum of change for a moment of diversion. It is perhaps accidental that their evolution coincided, for a period, with that of drama.

There was the nickelodeon, and then the storefront theaters exhibited a series of short subjects. The program lengthened and coalesced in an effort by the exhibitors to justify increased admission charges; as the unitary film approached an hour's length, a provenance was found for this new bastard art: It was, it was observed, not unlike the drama. And for the last eighty years the cinema has — except for the marginalized "short subject" — aped the staged drama both in length and pretensions. Both ran eighty to one hundred forty minutes and professed to explore the human condition. In its various humors.

But of late we see a divergence. Just as the history of religion is Moses' fight against the people's wish to reinstitute idolatry, and as our republic's history is the fight against the masses' wish to lay down the burden of representative democracy and cough up a king, so, finally, in entertainment we see ourselves, the audience, clamoring for a repeal of the laws of dramaturgy and a reversion to entertainment as pure titillation.

The pornographic and the mass-market Hollywood film string together titillating instances of sex, violence, and emotional exploitativeness — these instances separated by boring bits of nonsense called, in the trade, backstory, or narration. The contempt with which these interstices are treated is a reassurance to the consumer-viewer that better will be coming soon.

As an addicted movie viewer and old fogy, I have carped and carped at the ludicrous distortion of the dramatic form that movies have become, until, having fatigued first anyone who would listen and finally myself, it occurred to me that the Cinema is just going its own merry way, diverging from its momentary harness-mate, the Drama, and slouching toward Bethlehem like the rest of us.

"Alright then," "Nice butt, kid," and I close with my favorite scriptism: "Outside, the neighborhood looked like what just happened."

"It's Necessary
for the Scene"

It seems to me that the Theater has always been associated with sexual license. This may date from the days of the Greek mystery plays and their cult prostitutes; and it may, in fact, predate such shenanigans. We know that in the eighteenth century *actress* and *whore* were synonymous; and the Victorian novel catalogs this identity or prejudice's persistence into the next hundred years. The identification continues in the twentieth century in the dramatic character of the Libertine Actor and his Loose Sister, and we see the survival of the Victorian in the countless film reiterations of the Rich Man's Son lured by the Chorus Girl.

Now, what of it?

I've spent my adult life and a bit of my childhood in the Theater and have found it agreeably anarchistic as per sexual mores. The Touring Company, Stock Company, Film Crew on Location, is and considers itself a hermetic band, convened for the purpose of the Show and capable of making its own rules for most activities, sex prominent among them.

The rigors of a nomadic life and its frequently concomitant poverty and loneliness are balanced, and, I assume, have been historically, by various freedoms. We show folk, in my experience, have enjoyed our strangeness and consequent allure to the nontheatrical populace, and there you have it — one might step out, of an evening, with this or that Local, and no harm done.

But such took place, I say, *after* the show. *After* Ansky's *The Dybbuk,* or George Cohan's *The Tavern;* or *Twelfth Night,* or *Uncle Tom's Cabin,* or whatever: The hanky-panky went on *after* the show.

Part of the Player's allure came and comes from his or her personation of the Grand Figure. The Actor or Actress played the larger than life. They dealt, up there, with triumph and adversity, with failure and success; in short, with drama.

Yes, that is attractive. Who could blame the Johnnies of all sexes for waiting at the stage door?

But what of this new thing? What of the now-obligatory pornography in films that masquerade as Dramatic Entertainments?

In almost every film remotely construable as a Drama, we discover scenes of simulated sex, and I don't get it. And I don't like it. It's cheap, it's pointless, and it degrades the Players and the form.

Pornography violates the Aesthetic Distance. What does this mean? When we see the scene of simulated sex we can think only one of two things: 1) Lord, they're really having sex; or 2) No, I can tell, they aren't really. Either of the above responses takes us right out of the film. We've been constrained to remove attention from the drama and put it on the stunt.

It degrades the form. When you have to put the Plastic Frogman in the box of breakfast cereal, it means one of two things: either the cereal is no good, or it's indistinguishable from its competitors.

I, as a craftsperson, would be ashamed if either or both were true of my work.

And Pretend Sex is cheap. It's in bad taste; and if you look closely, you'll see that the actors aren't really doing it that well. They're self-conscious, and well they might be. For they are likely trying to hide their shame, or to keep something (physical or emotional) private, or they're trying to convince themselves that what they have been told is true: that their writhings are, in fact, essential to the film. They look uncomfortable because they are. They aren't acting — which they've, presumably, been trained to do — they're faking it.

And it's demeaning to the actresses. They get cajoled and badgered, subtly and not-so-subtly coerced into such vile silliness.

I have an actress friend who was convinced-coerced into doing sex scenes in her last three projects. Work is scarce, and all of us — in my profession and, perhaps, in yours — have ambitions. She did the three scenes; and only months later did it strike her that they were *television* films and the sex scenes couldn't be shown in any case.

And I am married to an actress. All of this "It is necessary for the scene" makes me a wee bit cranky.

How would you feel, sir, if your wife were a carpenter, and every time she bid on a job she was informed that, at periods during her work, she would be required to take her clothes off and pretend to achieve orgasm?

It makes me sick.

And you, Sleazy Producers — I wish you had all been born punched in the mouth. You panders. Have you no women of your own? For shame.

Now, I think movies have always been bad. And I adore them. I will watch the worst trash, happy as the aficionado/dolt that I am. I like 'em. They reveal, to our Wise Remove, each decade's foibles and prejudices. It's sad to see the Black Native Bearer falling from the mountain ledge and hear the White Hunter exclaim, "Oh, my God! What was *in* that pack . . . ?"

It's sad to see Lo, the Noble Savage, exploited in every ancient and contemporary film. It's sad to see the wacky women-hating comedies of this and other times, and the men-hating comedies, and *Gentleman's Agreement,* that brave film which teaches, as one wag had it, that we should always be kind to a Jew, because he might turn out to be a Christian.

Stanislavksy told us that we shout "Bravo" the same number of times in any season, regardless of what's on. We grade on the curve. We see the prejudices only of times gone by, and even then, only of others, revealed to us, perhaps, to make us thankful we have none of our own.

I think that Movies, with few exceptions, have always been trash. I would like to aver that this trash has, historically, been better spirited but, on reflection, I cannot.

It has not, however, been pornographic.

I do not think pornography equals rape. I do not think it begets rape, or causes the dissolution of the Family, or any of that tripe. I think pornography is the resort of disenfranchised men who are or feel deprived of healthy sex. I think that men in that predicament might seek out either healthy sex or legitimate pornography, instead of its ersatz reduction passing itself as Entertainment. It is, I think, fear and self-loathing that hamper either pursuit.

It was Hugh Hefner's genius to put naked floozies in a literary magazine, and to found a chain of high-class whorehouses that did not sell sex. That man got the Brass Ring. His clients could indulge in fantasy that was, though limited in potential, almost without guilt.

The consumer of our contemporary Aberrant Entertainment can, similarly, pay seven bucks to see such and such a global celebrity in the buff while assuring himself that he is watching a Drama; that, in effect, he "only reads it for the articles."

Well, okay. That's his business, no concern of mine, were it not that the Players are my Colleagues, and it's my craft being degraded. I prefer the arrangement where we kept the acting and the hanky-panky separated by the Stage Door, and they had to buy us dinner first.

The Jew for Export

Both the screen's first and latest heartthrobs — Theda Bara and Winona Ryder — are Jews; but how would one know if one did not know?

The position of the Jew as a minority in films is closer to that of the Gay than that of the Black; his or her identity is, to a large extent, capable of being either concealed or revealed.

There have been traditional, token, and stereotypical "slots" for the Gay actor (or, better, the actor representing a stereotype of Homosexuality): "allowed" or "quota" roles played by Franklin Pangborn, Billy De Wolfe, Grady Sutton; but the bulk of the actual Gay populace in the movies had to keep its sexual orientation to itself.

So with Jews. When they act, in films, in a stereotypical (weak, flighty) fashion, they are allowed to avow themselves as Jews (Leonid Kinskey, Mischa Auer, Felix Bressart). When, however, Jewish actors or actresses behave in a normal (i.e., "Jewish") fashion, they are co-opted as "universal."

Blacks were plagued by the caricature performances of Mantan Moreland, Willie Best, Stepin Fetchit, Butterfly McQueen; and only in the last fifteen years has the moviegoing populace seen African American actors in a large (i.e., "nonquota") number of straight-ahead, nonstereotypical roles.

This Coming Out is seen also in the recent not-for-export Gay films and portrayals: Hal Holbrook in *That Certain Summer,* Daniel Day-Lewis in *My Beautiful Laundrette,* Bruce Davison in *Longtime Companion,* Tom Hanks in *Philadelphia.* These roles and performances are not quota-filling sops to the liberal consciousness; they are the legitimate expressions by the writer and actor of his or her understanding of one aspect of humanity, in this case, the Gay Condition.

But we Jews remain in the closet.

Leslie Howard, Cary Grant, Paul Lukas, Kirk Douglas, John Garfield, Leon Ames, Melvyn Douglas, Edward G. Robinson, Lee J. Cobb, Paul Newman — all Jews — are considered "universal," and the only "Jews" one sees in the flickers are insulting stock portrayals (e.g., the nightclub owners in Spike Lee's *Mo' Better Blues*) that, if they pictured African Americans, would rightly get the theater picketed. The Jewish movie stars named above — and let me add to the bookends of Ms. Bara and Ms. Ryder, Paulette Goddard, Barbara Stanwyck, Sylvia Sidney, Shelley Winters, Judy Holliday, Lauren Bacall, Anouk Aimée, Barbra Streisand —represent a heroic literature of which we Jews can be proud and which we might emulate. But we could do so only at the cost of certain psychic assimilation. That is, we could be proud of the actors, but not without realizing (and, to a certain extent, endorsing) their "escape," as it were, from a Jewish identity. With the notable exceptions of John Garfield in *Gentleman's Agreement,* Rod Steiger in *The Pawnbroker,* and a few performances by Sam Levene, there are few Jews I recognize as Jewish in American films until the family in Woody Allen's *Radio Days.*

Jewish actors won acceptance at the cost of shedding a Jewish identity. Jewish scripts, similarly, came to the screen only in a sanitized version. (*Avalon,* Barry Levinson's beautiful film of his family's immigrant experience in America, has, as I remember, no reference whatever to the family's Jewishness.)

The screen's best love story, to my mind, is *Brief Encounter.* This story of an impossible love is, essentially, a homosexual tale — that is the Dark Secret of the two principals, and the reason they must absolutely part. It is that impossibility which imparts the unbearable poignancy of the film — it is a Gay love story told by a Gay writer, and cast in heterosexual form.

Similarly, the greatest American play, arguably, is the story of a Jew told by a Jew, and cast in "universal" terms. Willy Loman is a Jew in a Jewish industry. But he is never identified as such. His story is never avowed as a Jewish story, and so a great contribution to Jewish and to Jewish American history is lost.

It's lost to the culture as a whole and, more importantly, it's lost to the Jews, its rightful owners.

This is a case not dissimilar to that of the Native Americans, whose ancestors' bones were exhumed in the Black Hills, taken from sacred sites, and filed in the Smithsonian Institution "for the benefit of America at large."

It is as if Great Britain claimed the art of tap dancing as its own, and cited Irish clog dancing as its progenitor.

And who can forget Louis Armstrong, whom the dominant culture would not endorse as African American, but only as "Goodwill Ambassador to the World" — a phrase meaning "Honorary Aryan" — and Danny Kaye was another one.

I recently saw the film *Cool Runnings,* the story of the Jamaican bobsled team. In one scene a Jamaican lad is told by his father that a job is waiting for him in Miami with the law firm Windsor, Windsor and Cohen. The firm name is repeated several times, and each time the name Cohen is spoken, as it were, in quotes, lest we overlook the fact that it has been intended as a joke.

Why has a Jewish name been inserted for its supposed value as comedy? Is there something amusing in the name? It is thousands of years old, it is a Hebrew word, and it means "priest." I do not find anything exceptionable about it — save its use as a joke.

And I do not like *Schindler's List*.

It is to my mind *Mandingo* for Jews. *Mandingo* was a slave epic made for those interested in watching well-built black men being mistreated. *Schindler's List* is another example of emotional pornography.

It is not the Holocaust we are watching. It is a movie, and the people in the film are not actually being abused, they are acting out a drama to enable the audience to exercise a portion of its ego and call that exercise "compassion." *Schindler's List, Dances with Wolves, Gentleman's Agreement* — these films show a member of a dominant culture who condescends to aid those less racially fortunate than himself — who tries to save them and fails, thereby ennobling himself and, by extension, his race. This comfortable theme is more than a sham — it is a lie.

The *New York Times* has the charming habit of decrying the latest yellow journalism excess on the op-ed page. In the tabloids we find the scandal on page 1. In the *Times* we find it on the op-ed page. "Is it not deplorable," they opine, "that we are deluged with coverage of the ——— scandal; with facts like the following. . . ."

Similarly, *Schindler's List,* ostensibly an indictment of the German murder of the Jews, is, finally, just another instance of their abuse. The Jews in this case are not being slaughtered, they are merely being trotted out to entertain. How terrible. For, finally, this movie does not "teach," it does not "reach a great number who might otherwise be ignorant of this great wrong." It is not instruction, but melodrama. Members of the audience learn nothing save the emotional lesson of all of melodrama, that they are better than the villain. The very assertion that the film is instructive is harmful.

It is destructive. The audience comes to the theater in order to, and leaves the theater feeling they have looked down on actions that they have been assured — this is the film's central lesson — they would never commit.

This "lesson" is a lie. The audience is not superior to "Those Bad Nazis." Any of us has the capacity for atrocity — just as each of us has the capacity for heroism.

But the film panders to the audience. It invites them (as does any melodrama) to reward themselves for Seeing That the Villain's Bad; and, in the Liberal Fallacy, of feeling this perception is a moral accomplishment.

The mechanism of *Schindler's List* is that of "If you can't pay the rent, then I will tie your daughter to the train track."

The Nazis are the waxed-mustachioed villain, and the Jews are the daughter. The film is as far from philo-Semitism as concern for the girl on the tracks is from feminism.

Two jokes I heard in Israel: 1) There's no business like Shoah business, 2) Do you know why Hitler killed himself? He got his gas bill. Are these jokes revolting? They may or may not be, but they are legitimate attempts to use a dramatic form (the joke) to address the insoluble and oppressive phenomenon of genocide.

Schindler's List, on the other hand, is an exploitation film.

Art as a Helping Profession

It was, and still likely is, fashionable for the Valedictorian, in the better schools, to speak of the graduates' responsibility to Go Out into the World to Help. Students felt privileged and, therefore, both obliged and equipped to help. Their aid was going to be directed at those less fortunate than they were, and was to consist — if in nothing else — in their presence among those unfortunates.

How could the Graduates help but feel superior? They had been so instructed; that instruction, it seems to me, being something more than a by-product and approaching the totality of a liberal arts education. Such education might be parsed thus: You are arrived and are, so, removed from the Lower Classes. Proof of your election is this: You have not even been taught a skill.

Those so instructed sought and in large measure (until the late economic unpleasantness) found occupation that would support and divert them, but that was free of the taint of work. They went into the Helping Professions, which to a large extent were Government-supported (and, as important, socially supported) welfare programs for the Bourgeoisie.

Society can support with money and/or with status. But its highest regards of the same are made, as it were, in secret — so that they appear to emanate not from social will, but from the very gods.

At the highest level we see the superstar of art or politics lavished with wealth, coddled, and emulated, as if he or she possessed sufficient merit to deserve such treatment.

Down the scale we see the foundation administration, lauded and paid for Service to the Community, their reward scaled down, as their contribution is not free of the taint of "work."

At the bottom of the pile we have the Welfare Recipient, who performs neither work nor service, and whose recompense, therefore, is both meager and given in the odium of something called "charity."

In the middle of the scale are the Helping Professions: These folks are paid in status and coin for service to the Community. The coin is for their time, and the status is in relation to the degree that their time is considered spent in other than work.

The Helping Professions are not work in Mr. Veblen's

sense — they are of the status, or close to the status, of Honorary Leisure.

Also exempted are the Arts.

Once, almost in recent memory, a lower-class service (almost a menial job), the Arts have become, with the advent of the Mass Media and the growth of the Superstar, a Helping Profession.

Their status, and the status of their practitioners, has been raised. This has, of course, attracted quite a bit of riffraff to the arts. Folks who previously would have directed their efforts toward one of the other Protected Endeavors now call themselves artists. They do so because the arts offer the benefit of self-proclaimability, supported by almost universal unemployment.

For the influx of the untrained, unskilled, uninspired, and inexperienced to cast themselves as artists, however, requires a consensual change in our definition of Art. It was fine when art was an outré hobby for the amateur to "putter at," to daub at the canvas, to take voice lessons, to spend a few years in Bohemia. No one save the poor deluded — in the brief virulence of the bohemian illusion — expected to live a life that way.

But times have changed, and the middle class, like any other, must be subsumed and explained away, and if there is no occupation for them, such must be provided.

"Video art" replaces filmmaking. "Performance" replaces theater; "installations" replace sculpture.

These ersatz endeavors offer the practitioner a leisure activity validated by society — not because said validation produces any worthwhile product, but because it keeps the practitioners out of mischief and off the welfare roll.

Like the gold rush, this new and approved leisure occupation offers the near-irresistible "something for nothing." These pseudo-arts offer the fantasy of every amateur: that it is possible to pass from a state of pristine ignorance, devoid of discipline and skill, and become an Artist on the moment, through an act of Will.

Every adolescent beginner, every neophyte, every hobbyist, dreams of the "technique" pill that would allow the taker to avoid the unfortunate tedium associated with study. And lo, our new pseudo-arts require no preparation whatsoever. The practitioner can pick up his or her video camera and start making "art." Anyone sufficiently devoid of shame can parade about a stage performing sundry unrelated functions and call it "performance." Just like the Duke and the Dauphin.

There is a contract offered by such a practitioner, and it is a sort of Fascism: I, the performer, proclaim ART to be an exercise without norms, without strictures, and without antecedents. What I am doing is ART because I say so; and, as you are forgoing the enjoyment traditionally attendant upon viewing ART, I will offer you something else. In accepting my premises and my work you prove yourself right thinking, and, so, having seen the light, will be able to call your *own* works ART.

Perhaps such shenanigans are not prima facie evidence of irreversible Moral Decay, but, again, just Society preserving the social fabric by licensing otherwise antisocial behavior — much in the same way that what was once called vagrancy is now seen as homelessness.

But there is a price that society pays and will pay for "protecting its own." Our social norms become daily more general and more simplistic — more homogeneous — and dictated by the central censor, that is, the media.

The local journal, the regional school of painting, the coffeeshop theater, the small press, all shuffle off the stage.

The pseudo-artists claim the provenance of the avant-garde (and they are welcome to it), but in operation their work does not serve to shock but to strengthen the stolid aspects of society. They are, perhaps, the flywheel of the media, dissipating excess energy through *droit de fou*.

The pseudo-arts are not art. They are not the voice of an artist, or of a community, but (in their harmful aspect) a form of demagoguery. In participating in pseudo-art, the practitioner and the audience, acting as a mob, endorse the meaningless.

I am struck and, as many times as I have heard it, shocked by the *whooping* that seems to've replaced applause among the young at the end of dramatic performances. In this I see the audience *performing* enjoyment rather than expressing it. "Yes," they seem to say, "I have seen that to which I am entitled." But their expression is an animal noise, and it is false at that. The *whooping* is a proclamation. It is an arrogant and infuriated denial of the meaningful, of the individual, of the nonquantifiable — in short, of art.

For Art is not political (and what is more political than the cry "I say nothing has Meaning. Join me!").

Art is not educational, and it is ennobling only as and to the extent that joy may ennoble.

What a perplexing time and country. I have seen perfectly good blocks of granite ruined by having engraved in them dialogues from soap operas, said blocks placed, at civic expense, in the public parks and called Sculpture. I've heard of youngsters going on stage to gash their flesh, press paper over the cuts, and display the bloody patterns, and call it art. We have confounded the right of Universal Expression with the notion that everyone, therefore, must have something to say.

That a play is on an Important Topic does not mean that it is a good play. The play is not meant to "help." The artist is no more equipped to "help" than the deluded Ivy League Graduate.

Art is not meant to inform. It is a mystery. The true artist must, in these as in any other stultifying and confusing times, make his or her own way through both derision and subsidy.

And, of course, each age cherishes its own wretched delusions. That Art and the Artist have, in our time, become important is understandable as an economic correction. That the artist need not have skill, and the performance need not have meaning, that the audience need not have pleasure, these freedoms produce and will produce interesting aberrations as Society gropes its way back to the men and beasts in the Arena.

Demagoguery

It is interesting and frightening that the grosses of movies and plays are broadcast both as news and as an argument for their further financial success.

Hazlitt wrote that it is easy to have the mob agree with you, all you have to do is agree with the mob; and what is demagoguery other than the appeal: Everyone else seems to like it, do you mean to dispute them? It is no accident that television arose to minister to the postindustrial society.

There is little or nothing for a great segment of the population to do, and that little may be unrewarding, challenging, and creative of anxiety. In our time entertainment ceases to be an elective employment of leisure and has become a staple of existence — it is an analgesic/anesthetic and an apology for and to the postindustrial society — it is Marx's "opiate of the masses."

If food is nourishment the purpose of which is to fuel the body, it is not hard to choose the broccoli. If food is entertainment, who would not choose the french fries? The fast-food chains thrive through corruption of basic human need for nourishment into a need of entertainment.

The mass media likewise corrupt the human need for culture (an admixture of art, religion, pageant, drama — a celebration of the lives we lead together) and churn it into entertainment, marginalizing that which lacks immediate appeal to the mass as "stinking of culture" or "of limited appeal."

The information superhighway seems to promise diversity, but its effect will be to eliminate, marginalize, or trivialize anything not instantly appealing to the mass. The visions of Modigliani, Samuel Beckett, Charles Ives, Wallace Stevens, survive for the moment as *culture* in a society that never would have accepted them as art.

It has been noted that society can only choose her masterpieces from works that are known.

The synagogue- or church-basement theater, the small press, the barbershop quartet, need little or no corporate, government, or institutional approval to function. They are an organic outgrowth and expression of the ad hoc group, come together to share and create a vision of the world. The mass media — and I include the computer industry — conspire to pervert our need of community. They capitalize on the inherently hypnotic nature of the television screen, and they and we ascribe post facto rationale for our otherwise incomprehensible mesmerized immobility.

It is not, we say, that we have traded art, religion, and politics for an electronic toy, no, but rather we are becoming wise in electing to employ this organ of "information." We are told that the television, the computer, the interactive videos, the different versions of, finally, this toy, contain or will contain all possible *information*. In the reductio ad absurdum of demagoguery, we are told that we, in displaying the wisdom to sit in front of the thing, will be told all things — in effect, that we have become God.

We are learning to believe that we do not require wisdom, community, provocation, suggestion, chastening, enlightenment — that we require only information, for all the world as if life were a packaged kit and we consumers lacking only the assembly instructions.

This is, to me, terrifying demagoguery — the idea that all things are known and that we need not even know them, that their knowledge is contained in a machine to which we have access, should we feel the need. If we substitute the idea of an omniscient and benevolent dictator for that of the television-computer, the danger of our situation becomes fairly clear. A group can be transformed into a jury, which organism can potentially dispense justice; a group can be transformed into an audience, conspiring to both appreciate and, if I may, wring understanding from a play; a group can be transformed into an army, legislature, et cetera, and a group can be transformed into a mob.

The demagogue endorses the individual's greed and hatred, and calls the practice of these sins enlightenment. The demagogue arises in times of uncertainty and allays the uncertainty with a lie: It is not that the world is a difficult place, but rather that *some group* is conspiring against you — destroy them, and all will be well. Mass media and the television-computer are naturally evolved tools for the transformation of the group-as-audience into the group as consumers. To that end they, in the main, immobilize the viewer so that he or she can be sold something.

As the media come to dispense not only "entertainment" but politics and justice, as the poll replaces both the electoral process and trial by jury, as the computer replaces the library, we see the hypnotic tool's demand change from immobility to action. We are changing from a nation into a mob.

Self-Help

It is a natural process for awe to codify itself into religion. Religious institutions — as all organisms — desire, above all, to exist, to persist. So all religions are in the process either of resisting or of succumbing to the urge to become Priestly, Apostolic, and authoritarian in opposition to the force that gave them birth, i.e., the individual unstructured awe of God.

Worship degenerates into Religion, and thus into Drama, which decays into Entertainment, and then into Pornography, each step being an abstracted or decayed-developed expression of the individual's desire to *experience*.

Today's mind-cults, pseudoreligions, and — to a lesser extent — "self-help" forums present the participant an authoritative adult to listen to. They then reward obedience to this figure (or set of precepts) with the ultimate, secret fantasy of childhood.

In this fantasy the parent/teacher/mentor/book will reveal this: that one already knows everything there is to know, that it is not necessary to learn or to suffer, that every desire is right now within one's wish.

In this fantasy, the secret withheld from the Child — which he both suspects and doubts, which he wishes the parent to endorse — is that he is God.

Idolatry, of course, usually presents itself in the guise of Reason (or else why would we listen to it?). And the truly damned, as has been said, not only do not mind Hell, they are loyal to it.

For the organizations to which I refer offer a great boon: They allay anxiety, the sickness of the age.

They replace it with their approximation of the preverbal paradise of childhood, in which others do not exist; where the mother and father are felt as part of the child's body, where they are subject to his will, if only he will recognize it.

The failure to develop from this state (in the final case) is psychopathy, wherein the individual is actually not aware of the existence of other people as separate, discrete beings — where they are seen only as extensions of him- or herself.

The psychopath is responsible only to himself, for, to him, there *are* no others. His desires are not only the paramount, they are the only thing in the world.

The power of Idolatry is not that it suggests that the idol is God, but that the Worshiper is.

The very arbitrary and mechanical choice of the Golden Calf, for example, reveals its meaning: I, the Worshiper, have created you. I have abstracted you from myself. You were my soul (or "conscience," if you will), and I worship, finally, not you, but your absence.

The idolator loves the idol as we love the abscessed tooth when the dentist holds it up for our approval. We love it as it no longer plagues us. We are once again whole.

The Golden Calf, similarly, frees us mechanically from consciousness of our own egoism. It possesses no qualities either to chide or guide us. We have given it life. Much like the person who creates an imaginary Partner for his or her business firm — a partner on whom all blame can be placed for unpleasant decisions.

The Idol can be blamed, or can spare the individual, especially for those decisions that induce shame.

Magicians speak of a mechanism to free the observer — to enable him to accept that which, absent the mechanism, he would see as impossible. "Abracadabra," the wave of the wand, the puff of smoke, allow the spectator to accept or "believe in" the patently absurd. These offices permit the consciousness to "bow out" a moment, to say, in effect, "*Something* transpired. I don't know what, but some force greater than my understanding has interposed and brought about a surprising and delightful event."

The "magic" allowed us to do what we were reluctant to do.

Just so with *Der Führer,* and the Germans delighted

in him. He offered no power and no compulsion. He offered a mechanism to allow them to suspend their knowledge of the world and do what they knew was wrong. Adin Steinsaltz wrote that the human struggle to avoid strife, or to excise strife from our lives, is futile, as strife is our natural condition. That it is given us solely to choose the level at which we strive.

The continuum on which are found self-help, self-determination, and mind-control organizations rests on the proposition that strife derives from *error;* that the individual, in excising error, will come to that perfect state in which there is no strife — an idea as attractive in our age as it was in the time of the Exodus.

At the foot of Mount Sinai, in Freedom (adulthood) for the first time, the Israelites desired desperately to return to their preadolescent state. Being deprived of a pharaoh (parent) to worship or fear — being deprived of childhood — they took matters into their own hands.

They made a statue to allow them to worship the idol of any adolescent — to allow them to worship themselves.

The Recrudescence of the
Swimming-Pool Joke

Now, here is the reappearance of the Gun in the Pool joke.

Previously it was the man who called, and then the maid said, in a Spanish accent, " 'Ello," and the man said, "Who is this?" and she said, "I de new maid." The man said, "Where is my wife?" and the maid said, "Oh, no, Meesa, she upstair in de bedroom, her an' another man."

So the man now instructs the maid: Look in my study. You'll find a revolver in the table drawer. Go upstairs, shoot the both of them. The maid complies. He hears *bam bam bam* over the telephone. She comes downstairs.

"I shoot dem, what I do now?" she says.

"All right," he says, "now go outside and throw the

gun into the pool." There is a pause. "What pool?" she says.

That is the joke as everyone was telling it to each other two or three years ago.

And now a different group of people have discovered the joke, and, again, one hears it once a day, but changed in the particulars that follow.

In the current rendition the mistress is upstairs in bed with the gardener, and, after the maid says, "What pool?" there is a pause, and the man says: "Is this 641-8294?"

Now, if a popular joke is an example of the dream life of the body politic, must not the recrudescence of the joke be an attempt at mastéry-through-repetition? I think it must be. And that the addition of the telephone number and the addition of the gardener must then be an essential component, however superficial these changes may seem, of the attempt at mastery; i.e., if the joke, like the dream, is an attempt to explain/cleanse/restore order, then its reemergence must indicate that (just as in the case of a recurrent dream, or in the case of a compulsion) the first attempt was insufficient, that the prescription must be altered, and that we must try again.

The specification of the gardener is, at the least, an effort to draw the attention of the subconscious to the essence of the joke; which is, I think, an expression of racial fear on the part of affluent Whites.

In the joke, the fear, "my servants want to murder me," is inverted to "my servants think so much of me that, far from wishing me harm, there is no act that they would not perform on my behalf."

The teller of the joke is equal to the protagonist; that is, the unsuspecting (i.e., *untroubled*) male who simply wishes to speak to his wife. Danger from, and, in fact, the very existence of the Servants is the farthest thing from his mind, as is evidenced by the nonchalance with which the protagonist, and the lack of emphasis with which the teller, deals with the existence of the New Servant in the house. The fact of the New Maid is not remarked on at all; it is accepted both as a matter of course and, we may assume, as a historically not-infrequent occurrence. There is a new and unidentified person in the house, and it does not portend danger, it, in fact, portends nothing at all, for how could someone who called herself the Maid be significant?

Fear is also mastered, in the joke, by the bifurcation of the protagonist. The White Male protagonist is on the phone, and there is another unidentified (but, we would assume, equally White and male) man in bed with the Mistress of the house, and it is *this* man who is the victim of the servant — this adulterous, which is to say, guilty fellow who has called down upon himself the wrath of the downtrodden.

In the second attempt, the man in bed with the mistress is specified as the gardener; the joke didn't work at the first telling and is now being administered in a blunter form. The hidden content — fear of a revolt of the servants — is now more overt. Now the gardener copulates with the mistress of the house while a woman his presumably racial sister looks on. So now, with his death, the forces of Revolution, in his person, are given overtly what they "deserve." This change both acknowledges the servants' revolt and, having acknowledged it, insists on its punishment.

What about the addition of the telephone number? It is, it would seem, a simple effort to underline the "point" of the joke for those who were not paying attention. But *qui s'excuse, s'accuse,* and calling our attention to the fact that the entire encounter was a "mistake" points up the role of coincidence in the joke.

The joke concluded previously on a note of confusion — both for the protagonist and, I think, for the hearer: "What sort of ending is 'what pool' . . . ?" Pause. Pause. "*Oh,* I get it. . . ." The joke's glaring inconsistencies were glossed over by the effort of the hearer to make sense of what seemed, for the first scant moment, to be a non sequitur punch line, "Oh, there is no pool. Therefore, what? He must have the wrong house. . . ."

But the second telling attenuates the joke, sacrificing elegance for clarity (if the joke were to reappear again, the progression would likely lead to a punch line reading, "I'm sorry, I must have the wrong house"), and, in so doing, perhaps points to its true meaning, which is to say, to the problem it was created to address.

The joke is about fear (my servants want to kill me) and guilt (I manipulate them shamelessly and consider them mindless creatures), and addresses the question, "How can I live like that?" The addition of the telephone number, and the tendency that addition indicates, offers the answer. The answer is "You are in the wrong house," and the corollary, "Get out of the house."

The teller-protagonist wishes to divest himself of the trappings of wealth and race supremacy. He sees himself as put-upon by personalityless slaves who wish to harm him, he is quick to accept that his wife has cuckolded him, and, in the joke's inception, he has not even dialed his telephone number correctly.

Now, in the joke, as in the dream, there can be no "accidents." We must assume that he does not *want* to be in contact with his home; and, so, it is the insufficiency of the *first* attempt to distance himself from the unwanted environment, the wish fulfillment of dialing the wrong number, that results in the fantasy of revolt and murder, and (in the second telling) results in the simple, hopeless (and, now, conscious) reiteration of the joke's first thought/wish: to sever connection to a place that does not feel like home; and in both versions the gun is thrown/ordered to be thrown in the pool much as the burglar excretes on the house he has robbed, to foul it as a final and irreversible act of separation.

Cleansed by Death

Miss Manners informs us that it is craven to slight a politician with whose views or actions we do not agree when meeting him or her in a purely social situation. This delicacy is the only explanation I can offer for the liberal and moderate press's discovery and resurrection of Richard Nixon on the occasion of his death.

There is a common headstone inscription in the Victorian cemeteries in New England that reads: We shall not see him, but we shall meet him; and, indeed, as the one thing that doth befall us all, death might be called the ultimate social situation. And I am not so sure that Miss Manners would not understand it so.

But I choose to view it as a ritual cleansing.

The Torah states that all who touch the dead (with certain situations excepted) are defiled, and must cleanse themselves. New Orleans jazz bands march the dead to the cemetery with the slow-march of "Didn't He Ramble," but return from the City of the Dead to the beat of "When the Saints Go Marching In." The Irish have the wake, the Hindus had suttee; and, as we know, every culture has primitive rituals for dealing with this most primal of experiences. Here in the West, we clothe our primordial observances with nicety — as we once put skirts on the lamb chops — and we call it Culture.

Jewish tradition suggests, when visiting the dead, that we place pebbles on their headstones. This is not a simple calling card, but the wish, as is the headstone itself, "Stay down, don't come back." Our self-congratulatory liberalism in discovery of Nixon's "greatness as a statesman" is a similar wish. It is mastery through inversion.

His name was, in my family, among my friends and my peers, an epithet. His insistence on "Peace with Honor" in Vietnam disgraced the office of president and destroyed whatever moral strength our country may have had. "Peace with Honor" was an Orwellian phrase cloaking the desire of a man and his cronies to keep political power at absolutely any cost. Their actions sent tens of thousands of young men to die in an obscene and pointless war of adventure.

Nixon, and the Nixon White House, knew the war was wrong, pointless, and unwinnable. They insisted on continuing it, raping the economy and killing the servicemen, and called this insistence a quest for Honor.

They helped codify our unfortunate American redefinition of Honor as "the wish to be seen as right at all costs." Their vicious demagoguery destroyed the office of president and the American people's respect for the office. Twenty years later we live with an eviscerated electoral process that can focus only on the sex lives of the contestants.

The gluttonous greed of his administration and their backers, with their Good Republican Cloth Coats, turned us from a creditor into a debtor nation, and we'll be paying the bills for decades, if, in fact, we can ever pay them.

He lived his political life as main-chance brawler and mud-slinger. He was a red-baiter who didn't care whose life he ruined or what lie he told. He knew, as well as Helen Gahagan Douglas knew, that there was no "Red Menace," but he rode the red card to power and hounded the innocent to jail, to poverty, and to their graves.

He obstructed justice, suborned perjury and burglary. He resigned in disgrace. He traded his resignation to Gerald Ford in exchange for a pardon, and then lied and had Ford lie to deny the prima facie bargain. There was much talk, at the time of his impending impeachment, about "protecting the Office of the President" — such talk in support of the notion that the Office should not be subjected to the indignity of an impeachment proceeding. But the Office was not accused of crimes. Nixon was.

The notion that he should not stand accountable for misuse of the office of president because he was president comes close to a new definition of *chutzpah*.

His resignation, like the nolo contendere of his criminal vice president, was a plea of "guilty, but not contrite." The Senate's willingness to let him escape punishment was an affront to the American people; and, indeed, an insult from which our National Character (if there is such a thing) has never recovered.

We saw those crimes for which the Clerk paid and we were told that the Boss would be excused from any penalty. None of us is perfect. Rosemary Woods has taken her place with Teapot Dome. Life goes on, and we attempt to rewrite the trauma of the past under the heading *nil nisi bonum*.

Miss Manners is, as usual, correct and instructive — cautioning that the Public Person is owed, outside the orbit of his or her office, common courtesy. And yes, and yes, he opened diplomatic relations with China, and we are told that he played the piano, and could take a hand of poker, and swore colorfully, and was, in short, a man.

And it is not for me to speak of Nixon the Man; and it may, in fact, be craven to condemn the impotent dead. But reviewing his professional life, I have to say that he was a very bad man, indeed, and it is an act of wish fulfillment or worse on the part of the liberal establishment to say otherwise.

Make-Believe Town

What is this innocence that some have suggested was lost in the Oklahoma City bombing?

To suggest that the victims lost anything as amorphous, debatable, or of questionable value as innocence is to insult them and the survivors in their grief.

To suggest that those of us not personally touched by this tragedy lost anything at all is also an insult to the survivors.

A bomb went off. Some demented people planted a bomb, and others died.

Where, in this, is the Country-at-Large injured, and what is this innocence?

An old story has two men at a funeral. A friend sits next to a silent mourner, and turns to him after a while and says, "Why don't you let me share your grief?" The mourner replies, "If you were capable of sharing it, I'd gladly let you have it all."

The Talmud instructs that the only correct behavior in the presence of the bereaved is silence — we may infer that a solecism in the house of death may be both well-meaning and unwelcome; and that, in addition to being unwelcome, it may be other-than-pure, stemming from conscious or unconscious selfishness — if only the selfish motive to participate in the dramatic.

For the tragedy at Oklahoma City has undoubtedly attractive aspects for those of us not touched by it.

A television column in the *New York Times* of the period refers to "blood, gore, and anguish-stricken faces of parents . . . just the sort of television we want."

I call attention less to the quote than to the fact that it was never remarked.

Does the *Times* wish to suggest that we Americans, simultaneous with our "loss of innocence," *enjoy* the spectacle of families killed and maimed by bombs? No. The writer merely notes that *that's what we like on television,* where drama and actuality are confused and compounded into something merchandised as "news."

I tried to imagine an America reacting to reportage of the slaughter at Kent State that closed, "This is, of course, the kind of news we like"; I tried to imagine such a reaction to the carnage during the Tet offensive, or the assassination of Dr. King. Such a reaction would be, of course, unthinkable. Why, in this case, was it not even remarked — why is this event different? Why do we as a nation — and I beg pardon of those personally touched by the bombing, and of those who served and serve in its wake, but I do not think I can honestly use another word — why do we as a nation enjoy it?

We enjoy it because it fuses drama with the suggestion of personal danger — a danger we can enjoy precisely because we know ourselves to be perfectly safe.

We reduced the bombing to gossip, which appropriates the difficulties of others for their entertainment value.

We interjected ourselves into the play in the same way as the air traveler who reports, "Do you know, I was almost on that plane that went down. If I hadn't stayed in the hotel room to answer the phone, I'd have caught the earlier plane, and I'd be dead now."

All of us have heard and most of us have told such stories, and we know them to be false — to be exaggerations, transpositions, and inventions. We allow them to others and to ourselves in the name of drama. Finally, they are gossip about the Nature of the Universe, in which we accord ourselves — as teller or listener — a position much closer to center stage than circumstances warrant.

It has been said that the difference between a fairy tale and a war story is the one begins, "Once upon a time," and the other, "This is no shit."

Our country's reaction to the Oklahoma bombing was the war story of one in the rear echelon.

What is this "innocence" it's been said we have lost?

On first glance, it would seem to mean "a feeling of impugnity." But such a feeling suggests knowledge of and dismissal or discount of threat; and as such, it is antithetical to innocence. Threat may be discounted through knowledge, ignorance, or arrogance (which is knowledge disregarded). None of these three have anything to do with innocence.

Were we, prior to the fact, ignorant that bombing could take place? Were we aware but less-than-efficient in countermeasures? The answer to both must be no. The World Trade Center was bombed short months before; and what conceivable countermeasures could have prevented the Oklahoma City bombing?

Equally, what countermeasures could prevent a similar act of derangement? The counterterrorism bill is a flagrant piece of make-believe. It is under consideration not even for its calmative effects on a frightened populace — who do you know that's frightened? — but for its drama.

Our plea of violated innocence is made (to an audience of ourselves) for the happy feeling of righteousness it creates. One might say it is made equally to posit community with the bereaved, but its effect is otherwise, like the friend at the funeral who wanted to "share grief."

Our plea is also a dramatic confession of that *powerlessness* made popular by the twelve-step groups.

Alcoholics Anonymous creates out of the hopelessness and tragedy of alcoholism a community, and allows the individual to trade his or her feeling of helplessness and self-loathing for one of community, and so begin a cure.

The media's cry of Loss of Innocence was a similar confession, employed here, however, not as therapy but as entertainment.

We decry the militia movement and point to its delusions of persecution and conspiracy. It is easy to see in its adherents, as Eric Hoffer writes, "a lack of self-worth, a frustration, to see, that, the desire to escape or camouflage their unsatisfactory selves develops in the frustrated a facility for pretending." *

It is less comfortable to see the same mechanism at work in ourselves, who cry "Loss of Innocence," but the mechanism operates nonetheless.

The pronouncement posits — as do the militias — a mythical-perfect state that existed prior to the advent of the Savages (in their case, the government; in ours, the bombers). Both suggest an absolute, inalienable right: to kill in contravention of the laws of Society; to live free of randomness, in contravention of the laws of Nature; et cetera. . . .

I do not mean to equate the murder of innocent people with the solecism of mouthing platitudes — the acts are not equal. But the impulse is common; it is, to borrow again the thesis of Eric Hoffer, the beginning consciousness, on both sides, of Mass-Thinking. Hoffer writes, "All active mass-movements strive (therefore) to interpose a fact-proof scene between the faithful and the realities of the world."

The Michigan militia does it with reports of black

* Hoffer, Eric. *The True Believer: Thoughts on the Nature of Mass Movements*. New York, NY: HarperCollins Publishers, 1989.

helicopters, and the mass media do it with cant about loss of innocence.

The antiterrorism bill can no more protect against random violence than the reintroduction of the death penalty has protected us against murder.

Crime grows out of poverty, ignorance, and injustice. The disaffected, the misused, the oppressed, and the frustrated sometimes take their make-believe in the form of savagery.

What is this sense of "innocence" we've heard so much about? It may mean "childishness," or it may mean "protectedness."

The victims of the Oklahoma bombing were innocent of any wrongdoing. To say they are innocent is to acknowledge that they suffered and suffer tragically — through no fault of their own.

The Country-as-a-Whole did and *does* not suffer because of the bombing. This is not to say that we as individuals and as a nation do not feel empathy — it is very likely that we do — but, again, like that man at the funeral, we do not *suffer;* to suggest we do, in light of the victims' plight, is ludicrous.

One proof that we do not suffer is the antiterrorism bill. It is probably as a whole and certainly as a response to the bombing a make-believe remedy, and those in true suffering have no energy or time for show.

As we do not suffer we cannot claim a "sense of protectedness" as a definition of "innocence" — we would not claim loss of innocence after the devastation of a hurricane.

The other definition of innocence is *childishness*, and this, I think, comes closer to the mark. By crying "innocence" we allude to the mythical state of childishness, by which we mean "a sense of entitlement to freedom from care." But this is, of course, an adult formulation. No child is free from care; and so our plea to be so returned is a desire for a make-believe state.

The press, in its call for an imaginary past, and we, in mawkish attempts to co-opt the victims' tragedy, denigrate the present. We turn it into entertainment.

If both the past and the present are a fabrication, only the Future remains unsullied — the all-possible Future, in whose service all crimes are permissible.

Memory

When we were young my father would chastise what may or may not have been displays of ingratitude with tales of his life in the Depression. In the Depression, we were told, he sweltered in the City Heat for lack of the three-cent fare that would have put him on the trolley to the beach. We were told he ate rotten tomatoes and was happy to get them. And were we that deficient, we were asked, that even this instance of suffering was insufficient to create in us a state of gratitude?

And so we were labeled ingrates; but we reproached ourselves not with ingratitude, but with callousness. And we were angry. We were angry at those who demanded we "feel" a certain way about experiences of which we had no knowledge. That we control "feelings" over which we *had* no control.

It was not our parents' job nor their place to extort sympathy, or its counterfeit, but to act in such a way as to protect their children from want. To demand that those not involved somehow "understand" a difficult past accomplished nothing positive, and created resentment in those fortunate enough to have escaped the calamity.

That resentment grew, hydraulically, as it was repressed: We were commanded to feel something we did not feel, we grew angry at the demand, we wondered how we could be angry at those who had suffered, and so we repressed the anger, and it grew.

We were not, originally, angry at the sufferers. We grew angry at their demand. For they asked the impossible. Our feelings are not under our control. It is a false selfishness that counts the mechanical recognition of the appropriateness of sympathy as a good deed.

We all have felt the futility of trying to communicate our memories.

"Do you see that house? I used to live there," we say; and experience the myriad instances of joy, sorrow, and excitement with which the building — with which the mere mention of the address — fills us. But the listener can do nothing more than nod politely.

And even though we understand the mechanism — which prompts us to try to express, and which prohibits him from understanding — we may feel a pang of irritation. "Yes. But you don't *see*," we say. "That is where I first . . ." And still he can exercise only courtesy.

But what if we can relate the experience in such a

way as to make the hearer laugh or sigh, what then? If we can cast our experience in the dramatic form — then have we not communicated memory?

No. We have told a story, or have told a joke. In such a case the hearer relates not to our experience, but to the entertainment value of our performance. They, in effect, have an experience of Art.

This is the only instance in which the victim-hero of the reminiscence and those spared can react in a nonexploitative way — at a *performance,* which performance (to the listener) has *nothing* to do with the events that prompted it. His laughter at the punch line, his sigh or his tear, does not bring him closer to the putative event. It does not bring him closer to the days and the people that may have inspired the teller. It is a *new experience:* It is Art, and the hearer will remember it as such. His associations will be not with the teller's memory, but with the performance/joke/story/"installation."

For our experience of art is never modified — neither increased nor decreased — by the tag "based on a true occurrence."

And the viewer at the Holocaust Museum, at Yad Vashem, at any memorial to those with whom they are not immediately associated, can be moved by only two things: 1) Art; 2) their own capacity to feel.

Memorials — again, other than those of a personal loss — make a demand of the viewer "to feel." (They, in fact, *offer* this demand. It is the reason for their existence.) And this demand can be answered in two ways, each resulting in self-consciousness: It can provoke self-congratulation, "I can feel"; or it can provoke anger, "I cannot feel."

Memorials tend to attract those seeking out the former, and, so, like the Broadway audience that stands and shouts "Bravo" because they feel they have paid for it, participants at the Memorial tend to reward their effort with congratulation.

But it is a mistake to confound our happiness with a realized, complete experience ("Art") with sympathy. It is not sympathy. It is satisfaction.

Those who did not experience the Holocaust cannot "understand" it — no one can understand it. Those who suffered will continue to suffer, and those who did not can only wonder.

The survivors, in their anguish, require explanation, retribution, recompense, and can have none. They demand Memory. But the memory, for good and ill, will die with them. Nothing can re-create or duplicate it.

Horror arises every day; and our removed sympathy for its victims is nothing other than a capacity to be amused.

Minority Rights:

Jewish Kids in a Christian Country

Jewish kids are a minority in a country that has always been — disclaimers to the contrary notwithstanding — a Christian country.

The conflict over Church and State — the desire of many to eliminate mention of God and prayer from the public schools, for example — is more than a symbolic one to many American Jews.

"Prayer," to most fighting to "Keep God in the schools," means "Christian" prayer. This issue is not primarily one of theology but of racial sociology. The fight to keep prayer in the schools is a nostalgic battle mounted by Protestants, and is so understood by many American Jews, myself included. The nostalgia to which I refer is an affection for a religiously homogeneous country. It is a desire to return to that imaginary time when only one religion/race lived here, and in which time all citizens shared all values.

This longing for homogeneity excludes the Jew, as does the phrase "the Christmas Season"; as does, in fact, the construct "church and state."

It is not enough to say that the Jewish student may be excused from certain observances or that he or she should be questioned about possible racial slurs before any potentially exclusive activities are proposed. Both of the above, while well motivated and while presenting themselves as courtesies, are felt as racism.

It is the responsibility of schools to monitor the construction and content of potentially racially divisive activities to insure the protection of minorities. Granted, offenses and misunderstandings will occur in any case, and their airing and discussion can lead to better understanding.

The Jewish child growing up in an overwhelmingly Christian society labors constantly to assess correctly his or her role, status, and responsibility, and is often torn between the desire to belong to the dominant culture and the desire to remain true to his or her heritage, religious observances, and cultural identity.

Jews are a cultural minority in this country, too, just like African Americans and just like American Indians, etc.

The overwhelming Christianity of the United States is so ingrained as to be unconscious (in the most part) to the Christian majority; so that Jews, in many instances, in voicing an objection, are greeted with the attitude "Oh, come *on*. . . ."

Jews are told, "Oh, come on . . ." that the Christmas tree on the courthouse lawn is not a symbol of Christmas but is simply "a symbol of the spirit of the season" and so on. But it is only a symbol of the season if one happens to be Christian. If one is not, the assertion is more insulting than the Christmas tree, for it greets a request for respect with disrespect.

At a recent Martin Luther King Day assembly, an entire school acting in respect for the memory of Dr. King and in respect for the African American members of the community read poems and sang songs. One of the songs was "Jacob's Ladder," in which the refrain is "Soldiers of the Cross," and in which the singers assert that they will be good soldiers of the Cross.

A Jewish child should *not* be asked to sing that song, or any other song asserting Christian theology. It is possible to honor both Dr. King and the members of his race without singing religious songs. For example, the words of "We Gather Together" have been changed, and the new version is a staple of the Thanksgiving assembly.

Words to songs sung at the King or other assemblies should be similarly altered to expunge religious content the singing of which might be offensive to those not members of the religion that the song promulgates.

It is not only that the Christian assertion "We are soldiers of the Cross" is exclusive of the Jewish members of the chorus; the Cross was the symbol of the

Crusades, the Inquisition, and sundry other excursions during which Jews were slaughtered. For five thousand years the last sight many Jews saw in life was a soldier of the Cross.

The Martin Luther King assembly was deemed so important, and its observance in a respectful manner was deemed so important that children and parents were cautioned in memoranda to don "five-star dress." Can you sympathize with me and other Jewish members of the community who donned that five-star dress and then were treated to their children standing to sing a song that, in that setting, was offensive to their *own* race?

In Every Generation

I learned something about anti-Semitism today. I was reading about a disciple of Louis Farrakhan. The man was speaking at Howard University and spewing out hateful, violent, Jew-and-white-hating invective.

And I thought, "But surely if the audience (and, possibly, if the *speaker*) would reflect a moment, they would see that his accusations are preposterous." And I thought, "But surely the audience must know that we Jews have been the *friend* of African Americans, and traditionally the first and the most active white supporters of Civil Rights. If they would just consult the *record* . . ."

Two good, liberal, white, middle-class ("Jewish," if you will) responses.

But they answered a question for me.

The question was asked by Jews of my age in our teenage years and in our young adulthood. We turned to our parents and asked (of the Holocaust): ". . . but how could 'they' (or 'you') have let it progress? Didn't you see what was happening?"

And, of course, they had no answer to that rhetorical, accusing question.

This question was answered for me today, in my response to the newspaper.

My white-liberal, middle-class response to the Farrakhan hate mongers was the same as that of my brothers and sisters in Germany to the beginnings of Nazism: "You have your facts wrong. Now: If you'd bear with me one moment . . ."

Our error was this: Jew-hating is not caused by Jews. It does not arise out of a misconception. It does not even arise out of a need to hate Jews. It arises from a need to hate. We Jews are not the cause of anti-Semitism, nothing we have done caused it, and nothing we can do can cure it. We are just its approved victim.

We cannot cure it, and it is not only folly but self-destructive to try. We can only defend ourselves against it. Explanation, reason, and, importantly, *tolerance* in response to anti-Semitism are disastrous for us.

It is not that they will make the problem worse. They will not make the problem worse, but they will distract us from the danger of defenselessness. Reason is not a defense against anti-Semitism. The least appearance of race hatred is a questioning wedge whose end is murder.

Anti-Semitism is not ignorance, it is insanity —

human rage directed against a target deemed both allowed and unprotected. A woman cannot defend against the would-be rapist by quick access to Feminist reason. Rape is not caused by misapprehension. It is not caused by its victim. Neither is anti-Semitism.

I apologize to my parents for my sophomoric questions, and for interpreting their silence as ignorance or complicity.

The Torah says that Amalek will be with us in every generation. The jejune youth's question was, in the main, a wish that his generation would be spared. My parents' silence was courtesy.